The Films of Orson Welles

This book offers a comprehensive survey of Orson Welles's life and career, charting the progress of the extraordinary talent that produced such a sequence of splendid successes and puzzling failures. Robert Garis offers both an insightful account of Welles's fascinating character and ample interpretive commentary that freshens our appreciation and understanding of his work. At the heart of this book are sustained readings of Welles's masterpieces, *Citizen Kane* and *The Magnificent Ambersons*, and critically incisive accounts of his other major films, *The Lady from Shanghai, Touch of Evil, Othello, Macbeth,* and *Chimes at Midnight.*

Robert Garis was the Katherine Lee Bates Professor of English at Wellesley College. He published on a broad range of topics, including poetry, fiction, drama, dance, music, and film, and was the author of *The Dickens Theatre* and *Following Balanchine*. He completed *The Films of Orson Welles* just before his death in 2001.

CAMBRIDGE FILM CLASSICS

General Editor: **Ray Carney, Boston University**

The Cambridge Film Classics series provides a forum for revisionist studies of the classic works of the cinematic canon from the perspective of the "new auterism," which recognizes that films emerge from a complex interaction of bureaucratic, technological, intellectual, cultural, and personal forces. The series consists of concise, cutting-edge reassessments of the canonical works of film study, written by innovative scholars and critics. Each volume provides a general introduction to the life and work of a particular director, followed by critical essays on several of the director's most important films.

Other Books in the Series

Peter Bondanella, *The Films of Federico Fellini*
Peter Bondanella, *The Films of Roberto Rossellini*
Peter Brunette, *The Films of Michelangelo Antonioni*
Ray Carney, *The Films of John Cassavetes*
Ray Carney and Leonard Quart, *The Films of Mike Leigh*
Sam B. Girgus, *The Films of Woody Allen*, 2d edition
Jesse Kalin, *The Films of Ingmar Bergman*
James Naremore, *The Films of Vincente Minnelli*
James Palmer and Michael Riley, *The Films of Joseph Losey*
David Sterritt, *The Films of Jean-Luc Godard*
David Sterritt, *The Films of Alfred Hitchcock*

Orson Welles as Harry Lime in Carol Reed's *The Third Man.* (Photo courtesy of Photofest)

The Films of Orson Welles

Robert Garis

Professor Emeritus
Wellesley College

PUBLISHED BY THE PRESS SYNDICATE OF THE UNIVERSITY OF CAMBRIDGE
The Pitt Building, Trumpington Street, Cambridge, United Kingdom

CAMBRIDGE UNIVERSITY PRESS
The Edinburgh Building, Cambridge CB2 2RU, UK
40 West 20th Street, New York, NY 10011–4211, USA
477 Williamstown Road, Port Melbourne, VIC 3207, Australia
Ruiz de Alarcón 13, 28014 Madrid, Spain
Dock House, The Waterfront, Cape Town 8001, South Africa

http://www.cambridge.org

First published 2004

Printed in the United States of America

Typeface Sabon 10/13 pt. *System* Quark XPress™ [MG]

A catalog record for this book is available from the British Library

Library of Congress Cataloging-in-Publication Data

Garis, Robert, 1925–
The films of Orson Welles/Robert Garis.
p. cm. – (Cambridge film classics)
Includes bibliographical references and index.
ISBN 0-521-64014-8 – ISBN 0-521-64972-2 (pbk.)
1. Welles, Orson, 1915–1985 – Criticism and interpretation. I. Title. II. Series.
PN1998.3.W45G37 2004
791.43′0233′092 – dc22
2003055591

ISBN 0 521 64014 8 hardback
ISBN 0 521 64972 2 paperback

Contents

Illustrations

Foreword

James Harvey

Robert Garis was my dear friend. And he had, as he says of himself in *Following Balanchine,* a talent for friendship. He was generous and funny. Even before I knew him, he was described to me by a woman friend – no stranger to brilliance herself – as the one genius she knew. And though I might not have thought of quite that word for it myself, I came to know what she had meant by it. What Bob gave to his friends wasn't so different from what he gave to his readers or to his students. He distrusted the messianic almost as much as anyone could – but he had a messianic force in his relation to art. To hear him talk about a movie or a book or a ballet was to be invaded by the conviction of just how important, even *salvific,* art could be. Not everyone has that conviction – but to talk to Bob was to know it.

This is a marvelous book – a passionate response to a passionate artist. It's a genial passion: Garis is on the side of Welles – not at all condescending to him the way some of his recent biographers (David Thomson, Simon Callow) seem to do, in their dominating concern with the way Welles finally disappointed us. That he did so is probably inarguable, but – as Garis felt – it was the wrong emphasis to give to a career that gave us so much: *Citizen Kane,* for a start (was there ever such another?), followed by *The Magnificent Ambersons,* and later by *Touch of Evil.* Garis's essays on these films alone – with his account of Welles as a performative artist in the tradition of Charles Dickens (as well as John Ford and Sergei Eisenstein) – make this book indispensable. But then there are also his reflections on film noir, on Welles's commitment to Shakespeare on film, as well as a reading of *Macbeth* itself as multileveled and deeply persuasive as any account of that play I've read.

Garis is a major critic, as he showed not only in his two previous books

(*The Dickens Theatre* and *Following Balanchine*), but also in articles and reviews over his lifetime. This is the first of his books to deal directly and explicitly with movies, which became the consuming interest of his life toward the end. This book then is the culmination of that interest. And how grateful we must feel to have it. As with Welles himself, we could wish that the author had given us *more*. About *Chimes at Midnight,* for example, where the brevity encapsulates Garis's intensity of feeling about the film in a way that makes you long to hear more, and it's that intensity of engagement that you register – as the feeling behind his judgments, and behind this whole splendid book.

James Harvey is the author of *Romantic Comedy in Hollywood* and *Movie Love in the Fifties.*

Acknowledgments

Robert Garis loved to watch and talk about movies with his friends and colleagues. Prominent among the many with whom he both discussed the subjects of this book and shared draft versions of some of its chapters were David Ferry, Marie-Hélène Gold, Connie Harrier, James Harvey, Timothy Peltason, Lisa Rodensky, Margery Sabin, Paula Tagiuri, and Virginia and William Youngren. After his death, Series Editor Ray Carney, James Harvey, Timothy Peltason, and Margery Sabin collaborated in editing and preparing the manuscript for publication, with the painstaking assistance of Emily Coit, Jocelyn Cullen, and Emily Pellini, and with the generous financial support of Wellesley College. Richard Poirier gave early recognition to the project by publishing in *Raritan* a version of Chapter 3. Michael Gnat improved the manuscript not only by his expert copy-editing but also by his handling of typesetting and layouts, and his attentiveness to accuracy of detail. Beatrice Rehl of Cambridge University Press, through her helpful and sustained commitment, ensured the realization of the book.

I

Career Overview

The genius who made *Citizen Kane* and *The Magnificent Ambersons* in just two years in the early forties didn't go on to the smoothly developing career of productive growth and maturity that his admirers wanted for him and for themselves. There were great films later on – the last one, the sublime, simple *Chimes at Midnight,* and, before that, in a more brilliant, less natural style, *Touch of Evil* – and there were very interesting and entertaining not-quite-successes like *Macbeth, Othello,* and *The Lady from Shanghai.* A fantastic curio, *Mr. Arkadin,* was badly botched but vivid with temperament; no one but Welles could have conceived of it. Yet something, many things, blocked satisfying development. The failure was not in talent, certainly, but in control over the circumstances in which the talent had to work. But the talent did to some extent suffer in the process.

This was no classic trajectory of decline. *Citizen Kane* appeared in 1941 and *Chimes at Midnight* appeared in 1966, so we aren't dealing with an artist going dead, unable to live up to early promise. On the contrary, in some respects failure came with great rapidity. At the end of the forties, Welles was for the world in general a fascinating and famous artist who had produced two brilliant, perhaps great, films and a couple of very interesting ones; but already in the early fifties, he seemed to many people not just an artist who hadn't done anything important recently, but one whose career had gone seriously wrong, from whom nothing further was expected. At about this time, Walter Kerr, a drama critic and a coarse-minded bellwether of opinion, entirely self-appointed but influential nonetheless, said that Welles was "an international joke, and possibly the youngest living has-been."[1]

Then came the last act, when from *Chimes at Midnight* in 1966 until his death in 1985, he produced nothing – nothing, that is, that came to anything. He was constantly reported to be working on some new project that never appeared. Some see a pathological element in this behavior, but the style in which Welles carried it through almost suggests instead a modern echo of Dickens's Mr. Micawber – Welles was waiting for something to turn up.

Instead of retiring into the obscurity that would seem the suitably discreet setting for such failure, Welles became a prominent and popular figure on television, everlastingly on hand on variety and talk shows – *The Dean Martin Show, The Dick Cavett Show, The Tonight Show Starring Johnny Carson, The Merv Griffin Show* – and in addition keeping his face and immense bulk constantly before the public in the Paul Masson wine commercials he made into a legendary and cautionary feature of TV culture. He seemed in many eyes to have sunk as low as a major artist could sink. He himself didn't seem to share that opinion. He made these undignified appearances with smiling, benevolent imperturbability, without a sign of shame or anxiety or depression, and with obviously genuine and infectious goodwill and charm. He weighed some 350 pounds, and therefore might be thought quite seriously ill, but he made even this colossal bulk into a character and a performance. This long final chapter of the Welles story, the great film master who was producing no films, was lived out with bewitching grace, charm, and warmth. He was always a performer, and he had performed his nature and his talent with dash and flair in earlier days; in the seventies and eighties he performed his wit, his warmth, his size, his knowledge, his knowledgeability, and his memory of his unequaled past, with sedentary benevolence and, what is rarer, with an almost populist eagerness to please.

A tragicomic ironic note remains to be added to this image, for while Welles's decline as a filmmaker was being taken for granted in the world of show business, the virtual opposite was taking place with his reputation elsewhere. The growth of serious film criticism in the fifties and sixties in magazines such as *Cahiers du cinéma, Sight and Sound,* and *Film Comment,* the eminence of Pauline Kael's powerful writing in *The New Yorker,* and the growth of film study in colleges and universities – all these were steadily building up Welles's reputation as a master director. The fat, jovial wine salesman was the same man who had directed *Citizen Kane.*

As one examines the many starts and stops in Welles's career, the disappointments and self-betrayals, the great body of uncompleted work, there is no escaping the conclusion that something in Welles himself was making trouble. Many of the causes were obvious in Welles's nature from the beginning. His lifelong addiction to the performance of self, his ego-

"An almost populist eagerness to please": Welles with Dean Martin for a 1981 TV show. (Photo courtesy of Photofest)

tism and self-display, his lack of discipline, his recklessness, his lack of concern for contracts, or for other people – anybody who cares about his work has had to come to terms with these traits in order to take the full measure of his life or his art, for these traits were basic to his nature and behavior. They were also central to his art. If his performance of self was too often uncritical, and if for that reason it was a cause of the irregularities of his career, as it must somehow have been, nevertheless, performance of self was always the source, soul, and living center of his art. Everybody feels this, really, just as everybody feels it about another great performing artist, Dickens.

An artist can be called a performing artist when in each element of his work we feel in immediate contact with the artist himself and his intentions – trying to impress us, to show us his skill, to surprise us, to move us, to share his art with us. Dickens never wrote a description without calling attention to what he was doing: 'The master of description is now writing a brilliant description' or 'The master of eccentric characterization is now creating an eccentric character – and right in front of you.' When late in his career Dickens began putting part of his immense energy into dramatic readings of his works – Bill Sykes's murder of Nancy in *Oliver Twist* was the most popular and apparently the most hair-raising – it must have been because his hunger to perform his art for people could no longer be satisfied by performing on the page. He needed the audience right there, in person. It's not just a figure of speech to say that he killed himself in the overexertion of reaching for this contact. Dickens's thrilling readings were major exhibitions of energy and imagination, in comparison with which Welles's TV appearances may seem a dim and degenerate echo; but Welles closely resembled Dickens in practicing a mode of art in which we feel in contact, not primarily with an illusion of reality, but with the artist himself, the personality, the temperament, of the person who is making and sponsoring the illusion. You can't come within range of the power of such artists without responding, positively or negatively, to their assertive presence, their will to capture attention, to please, to astonish, to impress, often simply to make an exciting appearance before you. If such self-presentation offends you, this art is not for you.

To expect from such artists discipline and good behavior, to expect them to pay bills on time, live up to promises, keep to the budget, isn't sensible, and to use such expectations as a standard against which to judge them is simply to set a trap for them. Dickens himself happens to be an odd exception that proves this rule, for he was to all intents and purposes a man of great discipline and exceptionally controlled behavior, a hard worker, a family man, and all the rest. But although these accomplishments were movingly real, this ideal good-citizen behavior can seem but another part of the performance, as Dickens's lapses from this behavior in his treatment of his wife and children show.

With Welles, as with Dickens, performance of self wasn't exactly personal exhibitionism, though it may have been centered in it. Both artists were marvelously, perhaps supremely, gifted in the use of their media. Welles the person, in his mind and flesh, his personality, his temperament, above all his voice, was himself perhaps his prime medium, but he gave performances of self in the other media in which he worked as writer and director: theater, radio, and film, media for which he had an intuitive feel, and the mechanics of which he always mastered and deeply understood before he ever attempted performance. From an early age it was he who had the ideas and gave the orders in every enterprise in which he participated, but that was not only because he egotistically wanted to and needed to run the show (though he clearly did want and need this), but because much of the time he happened to be the only person on the premises who actually understood the machinery of the enterprise. The conception of Orson Welles as a romantically imaginative artist with an instinctive, intuitive feel for theater, radio, and film, is a right one, but so is another conception: that he was an artist who could be counted on for a high degree of sheer know-how and competence. It was competence as well as brilliance and charisma that won the cooperation of his professional colleagues even when what they felt toward him wasn't exactly affection or loyalty. To try to bring into focus his competence and his irresponsibility at the same time may be a good way to approach the Orson Welles puzzle.

For Welles's case offers more difficult problems about responsibility and irresponsibility than that of most artists. In 1892 Shaw paid a moving tribute to Chopin's sense of responsibility to his talent and his art, and in doing so sketched out what one might call the normal version of the issue, against which it is useful though painful to measure the ambiguities of the Welles case. Shaw was criticizing a biography of Chopin written by an earnest and very young man who was troubled by Chopin's failure to behave sensibly about money:

> To say . . . that Chopin was not a man to grasp opportunities merely because he did not jump at a chance of giving a paying concert, is to substitute the business standard of a smart agent for the artistic standard of the critic of a great composer. A man who died of consumption at thirty-nine and yet produced what Chopin has left us, was clearly a man of immeasurably greater energy and practicality than the late Mr. Jay Gould, who worked far longer than Chopin, and produced nothing.[2]

The clarity of Chopin's sense of priority contrasts painfully with the confusion of Welles's career.

Responsibility to one's talent, like Chopin's, is one thing at issue with Welles. Responsibility to people and institutions, and to one's commitments to them, is another. That kind of responsibility lies between duty and loyalty; it involves learned moral behavior but also the ability to imagine other people's wants and needs and an interest in doing so. But it's hard to be sure what responsibility to one's talent really means and to what extent moral considerations should come into play when responsibility to one's talent is the issue. Welles's responsibility to his own talent and his own work is hard to separate from his responsibility to the organizations and people with whom he was involved. And it is hard too to separate Welles's lack of responsibility to his talent from his susceptibility to other kinds of failure – of nerve, of self-confidence, of invention, of imagination. Throughout his career Orson Welles seemed to admirers and detractors alike to be tragically implicated in issues of responsibility, and it seemed to them tragic too how little steady awareness of this he showed.

The mix of self-performance and competence in Welles began early in his childhood in Kenosha, Wisconsin, and in Chicago. He was a show-off from the start, like a lot of other children; but the nervous energy, concentration, and focus of his showing off suggested from the beginning something exceptional in process. He was deeply attached to his mother, for whom art was a major passion, though she was not particularly talented or even well-informed about it. Long after her death she remained an important person in his life; it was for her pleasure and to win her attention that he had given his earliest performances. It may in fact have been because his mother was his first audience that he discovered the excitement and especially the rewards of the performance of self. He used to stand on a chair and pretend to conduct an orchestra, and he put on complicated shows with the magic set and toy theater his godfather had given him. This fairly ordinary childish behavior might have led anywhere or nowhere, but Welles's early self-performance seems always to have been tied to self-education; while he was showing off by playing these games he was at the same time figuring out how they worked, so that his fun with the magic set and the toy theater turned out later to have been the beginning of serious apprenticeship.

He showed the first fruit of the apprenticeship at the age of twelve, when he entirely dominated the theatrical enterprises of his school. Welles's parents had chosen the Todd School for Boys in Woodstock, Illinois, for him because they had sent his undisciplined and unfocused flop of an older brother, Richard, there for correction when it was still almost a military academy of discipline. The correction had worked to some extent, but that doesn't seem to have been the reason Orson was sent, and by the time he arrived the school had been transformed by the new headmaster, Roger Hill. His style was almost the opposite of severely disciplinary: indulgent, highly cultivated, and imaginative, but also shrewd and tough. Hill regularly sanctioned what a more anxious headmaster might have prohibited. It was he who allowed Orson complete control over the school theatricals for several terms, instead of insisting that the task and the honor be spread around in a more acceptably democratic manner. The trust paid off, for Welles's control of the Todd theatricals was deep and detailed to a degree amazing in a schoolboy. Welles's hard-to-please biographer, Simon Callow, who can hardly bear to acknowledge Welles's mastery in his adult ventures, enjoys describing Welles's boyish omnicompetence at Todd:

> Welles was dealing with kids, not merely untrained but not necessarily even talented. He was their own age, yet they took it, apparently without demur. It can only be because they acknowledged that the results justified it. During his time at Todd, Welles devoted himself to the theater to such an extent that it almost became a theater arts degree course – except that he was the teacher and pupil, course director and apprentice. He mastered every aspect of production during this time – design, stage management, lighting design, set-building. The campus theater was a well-equipped two-hundred seater, with a reasonable number of lamps, all on dimmers; a plaster back wall which made possible "realistic and stunning outdoor effects"; an arras, with a drape setting (the drapes being removable) and a rigging loft equipped with ten sets of lines. He used every aspect to its utmost potential. . . . He had, at this astonishingly early age, a clear conception of the unifying role of the director.[3]

One gets a vivid sense of watching Welles at play with the machinery of his medium in the élan of his first films, and indeed in all his films. Welles always wanted to get more than fun out of his new toys – he wanted to find out how they worked and what he could do with them. Along with play went concentration and purpose, qualities that in their completed development are richly visible in the finish and fullness of his great films. Welles's mastery of the machinery of his school theater was probably as much a matter of instinct as of diligent discipline, but that had been the case with Dickens, too, and with many other performing artists. Welles knew all about his own competence and delighted in it. When he boasted about it to Barbara Leaming, his least skeptical biographer, you can tell he knew how outrageous he was being, yet the frankness of tone is lovely, and the details of the boast compel belief. He was a virtuoso liar all his life, but he could also be a movingly sincere egoist:

> See, the one thing on which I am totally without self-doubt is the technical side of the theater, radio, and movies. And I never did anything that wouldn't work. I did things people didn't *like*. But any story you hear about something not working: *not true!* I am the only director in the world that I've ever heard of, or anybody that I've ever talked to has heard of, who comes on a set and puts his closed fist in a certain position in the air: *this will be a 40, right here.* Without a viewfinder, without anything – and I know exactly what will work. I am the absolute technical master of the medium. I have no shame in saying it. So if

people say something doesn't work, they don't know any better. That's all I can say.[4]

Instinctive mastery of the medium to some degree deserted him later in his life, conceivably because he got fewer and fewer chances even to touch the machinery.

The triumphs at the Todd School were followed by a series of lucky opportunities on which he seized with such speed and implemented so fully that they can be called his creations – genius plus competence, again. There's something like magic in the opening of Welles's career, though perhaps it's just the strength and certainty with which he believed in himself, and presented and performed himself.

Somebody – possibly Hill, most likely Welles himself – concocted the plan for Welles to go to Ireland entirely on his own at the age of sixteen, a seemingly unmotivated act that proved to have serious thinking and planning behind it. Somehow Welles had come to feel the glamour of literary and political Ireland. His teachers at Todd helped, probably, yet for a sixteen-year-old in Chicago in 1931 to try under any circumstances to explore and bring to reality such an intellectual discovery was an act of genius in itself. He got off the ship at Galway, instead of continuing to Cobh, and proceeded through the West Country to the Aran Islands and then to the Gate Theatre in Dublin, where he staged a major and thoroughly rewarding self-performance and self-creation. He wangled his way, as a gofer and intern, into this young company, which had been founded only five years before, and then, on the shaky basis of this minimal status, asked to audition for the long and important second lead in the upcoming production, an adaptation by Ashley Dukes of Feuchtwanger's *Jew Süss*. Despite the theatrical know-how he had gained at Todd, he had had no experience in the professional theater, and Hilton Edwards and Micheál Mac Liammóir, the joint managers, knew as much, but they had a role to fill, and Welles had already won them over with his energy and presence. Edwards told Welles immediately after his audition that he had been "bloody awful," which seems to have been a complicated compliment, for the audition actually seemed to both directors to have held great and complex promise. Mac Liammóir's brilliant memoir shows and explains his excitement about the occasion:

It was an astonishing performance, wrong from beginning to end but with all the qualities of fine acting tearing their way through a chaos of inexperience. His diction was practically perfect, his personality, in spite of his fantastic circus antics, was real and varied; his sense of passion, of evil, of drunkenness, of tyranny, of a sort of demoniac authority was arresting; a preposterous energy pulsated through everything he did. . . . And that was because he was real to himself, because it was something more to him than a show, more than the mere inflated exhibitionism one might have suspected from his previous talk, something much more.[5]

He got the role and had a personal triumph in it; the reviews singled out the sixteen-year-old boy almost embarrassingly for special praise. He had earned his place as a bona fide member of the company for the rest of the season, which ended with another happening that may count as a Wellesian magical conjuration, for the play scheduled for the end of the season turned out to be what always has had talismanic force and implication for theater people, *Hamlet,* in which Welles (still only sixteen) got to play – not Hamlet, to be sure – but both Claudius and the Ghost, getting some bad reviews for Claudius but some very good ones for the Ghost. In less than a year at the Gate, he had fashioned out of energy and belief in himself a solidly structured minicareer in the Irish theater.

What Mac Liammóir saw in that audition was not only raw talent and personality, but also the result of some form of discipline. "Practically perfect diction" on the part of a sixteen-year-old Midwestern American had to have come about through a more or less orderly process of self-shaping. Granted Welles's temperament, the process might have *looked* impetuous and instinctual rather than careful and painstaking, might have seemed closer to imitation, even mimicry, than to drill; but that is how this very young man's nature functioned and how it was to continue to shape itself. Mac Liammóir's stern description of Welles's performance of self offstage – "mere inflated exhibitionism" – usefully puts into relief his capacity to transmute "exhibitionism" into controlled performance in the medium of theater.

Luck was instrumental again in Welles's next career step, a chance meeting at a party back in Chicago with Thornton Wilder, at that time a major player in American cultural life, even before *Our Town.* Welles was in moody doldrums about his career (his mood perhaps another precocious self-performance of a would-be theatrical professional), but Wilder surprisingly turned out to know a lot about the Dublin triumph, which had got only "local boy makes good" attention in the Chicago press. In fact, entirely on the basis of the Gate Theatre's guarantee, Wilder offered Welles the magnificent gift of a career introduction to his good New York friend Alexander Woollcott, the critic and radio personality, one of the most powerful figures in the American theater. Woollcott in turn introduced him to his own great friends, Katharine Cornell and Guthrie McClintic, virtually the queen and king of the American theater in the thirties. They were then casting, in that summer of 1933, a small repertory company for a national tour to perform *Candida* and their latest hit, *The Barretts of Wimpole Street,* and to make their first attempt at Shakespeare with *Romeo and Juliet.* As at the Gate, it was after only the most perfunctory auditions that Welles was invited into the company. This can't have been as unprofessional an action on McClintic's part as it sounds. Welles had come to McClintic's attention through the kind of old-boy network now much distrusted, but McClintic was an experienced networker, who knew perfectly well how to further his own interests by these means. He couldn't have hired Welles so quickly if he hadn't been impressed by him – by his gifts and by the self-confidence with which he used them.

What McClintic saw in this audition must have been akin to what we see in the early films. At eighteen, Welles seems to have been, in everything that goes into the fashioning of a theatrical presence, essentially the actor we know from, say, the image of the youthful Charlie Kane in the first newspaper office scene in *Citizen Kane.* The height and bulk (just slightly odd in its awkwardness without seeming peculiar), the self-command, the almost comically chubby-cheeked and faintly Asian handsomeness that was yet undeniably handsomeness, the witty eyebrows – all this was fully formed and in force. Above all there was the voice, which had developed early and remained unchanged until he died. It was in the deployment of this voice that Welles's performance of self chiefly and most vividly took place. The voice was unusually loud and penetrating; many noticed and responded to a certain powerful "vibration." As one can hear at many moments in the films, he loved his own competence in using that voice for high eloquence in strong rhetorical patterns, for which he was equipped with a wide range of volume, nuance, and color, all under flexible control; he was also capable of and fond of bombastic roaring. But there is a more original and potent aspect to Welles's voice than eloquence: a seductive tonal undercurrent that is hard to fix because it plays in and through many other tones. At its toughest and most brilliant this tonal undercurrent expresses an almost cruel, cutting insolence, yet one that is seductive because we are invited to share in the power of the insolence and because we very much want to; we also want to share the voice's sly tone of amusement, a teasing, exciting complicity, even though it may be at something we don't quite understand. Almost whatever the subject, Welles's voice takes an ironic tone toward it, often with little discernible intention of doing so – not discernible, you feel, even to Welles himself. The irony is often free-

wheeling, though no less interesting and effective for that. Governing all these resources and centered in his voice is a confident lordliness, a lordly confidence invigorating and inspiriting when it manages to avoid condescension, which it does surprisingly often, though hard to take when it does not. This play of tone is the heart of the self Welles performs, and for all his studied eloquence and insolence, it really is play, a high form of play, and in its variety and in its unmistakably personal identity, it is an act of life in itself. It served him well in his whole career in the theater and film. We in the audience know the tone as the voice of the actor in performance, but it is easy to imagine how effectively and persuasively it operated as the voice of the director in rehearsal.

In the Cornell–McClintic company Welles's acting and behavior both pleased and annoyed his colleagues and was only half a success, nor did he in fact learn much from the experience. He was cast against temperament and physique as Marchbanks in *Candida,* certainly against Shaw's elaborate orders in the text, but the figure he cut seems to have gone over well enough and pleased McClintic, who doesn't seem in the least to have thought he made a mistake; Welles did indeed prove useful. The minor role of Octavius in *The Barretts of Wimpole Street,* on the other hand, bored Welles, who gave it almost no attention and did badly in it. There were other problems about his colleagueship. It was into Mercutio that he put his energy and imagination, and here too there might seem a mismatch of temperament between role and actor, with Welles's tone seeming a bit heroic for Mercutio's fantasy; but his conception and performance appear to have been convincing. Later in the long tour, the hazards of repertory conditions came into play when Brian Aherne joined the company to play Robert Browning; he was a big enough name to command the role of Mercutio as well, and Welles was sidetracked to Tybalt instead. He was dissatisfied with the change, and his Tybalt got relatively little attention in the press. But luck was in force again, for Welles's animal power in this role struck with admiration, even fascination, a key member of the audience, John Houseman, who became the instrument of an uneasy but extremely fruitful professional relationship that lasted through the making of *Citizen Kane.*

Houseman was a Hungarian, educated chiefly in England, who had gravitated to the American theatrical scene after rather unfocused experience beforehand. He was a past master at landing on his feet and something of a genius at forming artistic attachments with a binding personal element. He had come to know Virgil Thomson a bit socially, and on the basis of this very slight acquaintance Thomson asked him to direct one of

the milestones of avant-garde theater in America of the thirties: the Hartford performance in 1934 of *Four Saints in Three Acts*, an opera that the composer had written in collaboration with Gertrude Stein. Thomson didn't like Welles very much, but it was through Thomson that Houseman and Welles got other key assignments and made other key choices in careers that were now moving swiftly. The list of dazzling and original theatrical events that Welles and Houseman put together in the next three years of Welles's career is still hard to believe, though it has become familiar knowledge. These years have entered theatrical mythology as the model of what the beginning of a brilliant career looks like. This phase of Welles's career, with his creative energy at its height, his success with the critics, and the unceasing publicity with which his productions were received, continued almost unbroken until the late forties in Hollywood. For that brief period Orson Welles was the most famous man in American theater, and many thought he was the most brilliant.

It all started in 1935, when Hallie Flanagan asked John Houseman to run the Negro Theatre Project, part of the New York branch of the Federal Theatre Project, which in turn was a branch of the Works Project Administration that Roosevelt had recently inaugurated; Houseman naturally made his partner and protégé, the twenty-year-old Orson Welles, director, and Welles chose as their first production an all-Negro *Macbeth*.

Welles's *Macbeth* was in many ways a one-man show. His relation to his cast seems to have been a far from self-effacing or even selfless Wellesian performance of all-controlling directorial virtuosity. But the self performing, self-delighting Welles nevertheless turned in an impressively competent job. Houseman, admittedly no disinterested observer, gives a vivid and generous account: "He had the strength but also the kindness and loving patience – and a capacity for total concentration. He kept them going by the sheer force of his personality. His energy was at all times greater than theirs; he was even more mercurial and less predictable than they were."[6]

Welles's *Macbeth* for the Negro unit came to be called "the 'voodoo' *Macbeth*," appropriately enough, since its basic conception had been to give Shakespeare's witches new theatrical life as voodoo witches, and to give the play contemporary relevance by making a loose analogy between the action of *Macbeth* and events in the history of Haiti. This modus operandi, a foretaste of the theater of high concept with which we are now occasionally blessed and much more often cursed, remained his method in the three further great successes he achieved when, after *Macbeth*, he was put in charge of a division of the Federal Theatre Project called

Welles in 1936 directing Joseph Cotten and Arlene Francis in *Horse Eats Hat* for the Federal Theatre Project. (Photo courtesy of Photofest)

the Classical unit but known to insiders as Project 891. The first season opened surprisingly but, for many, effectively with a farce called *Horse Eats Hat,* an adaptation by Edwin Denby and Welles of Labiche's *The Italian Straw Hat;* this oddity was followed by the more traditional choice of Marlowe's *Doctor Faustus,* with Welles as Faust and Jack Carter, who had been the Macbeth, as Mephistopheles. During a lull, Marc Blitzstein's leftist opera *The Cradle Will Rock* came to Welles's attention; it had been highly successful in an earlier production, and in the Welles version it got an accidentally brilliant send-off through the publicity surrounding its touch-and-go premiere. Just as the opera was ready to open, Washington decided to cut back drastically on the funding for all branches of the WPA, and *The Cradle Will Rock* was ordered not to open. To show they meant business, the administrators of the Federal Theatre demanded that the theater where the opera was to play, the Maxine Elliott, be locked up on the day of the premiere, together with all the scenery and props – a variety of "lockout" that, ironically, expressed hostility toward the unionism that was precisely the subject of Blitzstein's opera. As the company waited outside the locked theater until curtain time, hoping for some last-minute miracle, a miracle did in fact arrive, thanks to the master magician. Seeing the performers eager to work, and the capacity audience eager to be entertained, Welles had the idea of putting the show on in a nearby empty theater (the Venice was chosen), without scenery or props, and obeying the rule that the actors, because of the union response to the lockout, were forbidden to set foot on the stage. Since the musicians too had been forbidden to play by their unions, Welles concocted the idea that Blitzstein should play the score on a piano, while the cast, dotted throughout the audience, should stand up in their places to act and sing their parts. This sufficiently bizarre plan was put into action, and was, as may be imagined, immensely successful – it was an occasion people would have given their eyeteeth to have attended. Welles's reputation as all-purpose master of theatrical know-how was established more solidly than ever.

Welles and Houseman soon broke away to form the Mercury Theatre, whose key productions were the modern-dress and by implication fascist *Julius Caesar* and Thomas Dekker's *The Shoemaker's Holiday;* these, together with the voodoo *Macbeth* of the Negro unit, were Welles's great achievements in the period. Meanwhile, again virtually by magic, Welles's talent for radio had been discovered, and he was exploiting it to the utmost. He started out in dramatized episodes of *The March of Time,* playing a wide range of characters, from the German president, von Hindenburg, to all five of the Dionne quintuplets, and his ability to handle such assignments eventually brought him offers from all the studios, so that he became, as he himself reported it, "one of the most successful radio actors ever," though also "unnamed, anonymous."[7] The excitement of these years must owe something to the staggering pay (a thousand dollars a week, more or less, in the middle of the Depression) that Welles was collecting for the fairly casual attention he paid to his activities on the radio, and which he was generous in spreading around among his colleagues. His energy and generosity made his talent for radio otherwise useful to his colleagues, for he took them along with him when he founded and directed the *Mercury Theatre on the Air,* which produced mainly serious middlebrow radio dramas. It also produced the notorious *The War of the Worlds,* a play that purported to be a news flash about an invasion of aliens from outer space, and fooled hundreds of listeners, particularly in New Jersey, into fleeing their homes.

The brilliant performance of self, inventiveness, skill, and competence of Welles's years in the theater and radio crested in *Citizen Kane*. Welles had been brought to Hollywood by George J. Schaefer, head of RKO, expressly to bring about this climax. It is doubtful that Schaefer had any concrete sense of Welles as an artist or of what sort of film he might be expected to make; signing him up was a business gamble of acquiring the hottest property around. Welles had had no experience with film, but had publicly announced that he was interested in learning, and the publicity surrounding his name made Schaefer take the chance of hiring him. Soon after Welles arrived he began looking for a screenwriter, and found a highly experienced one, Herman J. Mankiewicz, then more or less on the sidelines if not the skids because of erratic behavior, professional and private. Welles quickly formed an alliance with him, and together they worked out the subject for Welles's first film: the life of an American public figure, told from various points of view, to be called *American*. Mankiewicz was sent into isolation to write the scenario, accompanied and guarded by Houseman, who kept him from drinking and gave him intellectual company. Welles had been allowed to bring his Mercury troupe with him to Hollywood, and he soon acquired in addition an entire staff of the highest quality: Gregg Toland, one of Hollywood's master cinematographers, who had volunteered to work with Welles; Bernard Herrmann, the composer, who had worked extensively with Welles on radio; and Perry Ferguson, a highly regarded art director, with whom Welles got along exceptionally well. Welles's contract allowed him more freedom as a director than Hollywood had ever known, a tribute money was paying to genius, in hopes of the masterpiece to be produced. The most important of the unprecedented privileges was the right to final cut. Under such circumstances, the making of a masterpiece certainly seemed possible, and a masterpiece was in fact achieved.

Citizen Kane was at first gratifying to Schaefer in all the ways for which he had hired Welles – it had intellectual class, it was bold, original, and iconoclastic in both subject matter and technique. Granted these qualities, and granted the canny publicity accompanying its making, *Citizen Kane* seemed headed for major commercial success. But all of its virtues could never make up for the damage soon to be done to it by William Randolph

Hearst's violent attack on the film for what he called its libel of his mistress, the former movie star Marion Davies. Davies was a clever and talented woman, quite unlike the dim and mainly humorless Susan Alexander, the equivalent character in *Citizen Kane;* and there are reasons to think that Welles and Mankiewicz's chief target was Colonel Harold McCormick, the Chicago press lord, and his mistress, the ungifted opera singer Ganna Walska, for whom he divorced his wife, Edith Rockefeller, and built the Chicago Opera House. But many details of the film matched Hearst and Davies better than McCormick and Walska, and in any case it was Hearst who made trouble. Hearst's abuse of power in the media had qualified him as the ideal target for Welles and Mankiewicz's attack, and they now felt the impact of that power directed against themselves; the episode was a real-life cautionary tale, with a touch of black magic about it. Hearst's hostility, furthermore, was conceived in Hollywood to be a threat not only to Welles personally and to RKO but to the whole industry, not unreasonably, since Hearst controlled so wide a range of public opinion; the perceived danger was such that Louis B. Mayer and other studio heads actually went to the length of offering to pay Schaefer to destroy the film. Schaefer refused, partly perhaps because the controversy at the beginning seemed like promising publicity. But no businessman in the movies could have welcomed the sustained trouble Hearst eventually caused, blocking the showing of *Citizen Kane* in city after city, and costing RKO considerable money from lost box-office take and lost prestige. Nor did the bad publicity in the long run arouse much curiosity in the movie audience, for when *Citizen Kane* was finally exhibited throughout America, its success was only moderate. Since then, of course, it has far outweighed in prestige and admiration what RKO lost in money, and eventually it became a modest moneymaker itself.

Later in 1941, in the discussions between Schaefer and Welles about Welles's next movie, an adaptation of Booth Tarkington's *The Magnificent Ambersons,* Schaefer must have been influenced by the trouble *Citizen Kane* had run into, as well as by its poor performance at the box office, for he changed the liberal contract under which *Citizen Kane* had been made. Welles's right to final cut was taken away, a change important in itself but also because it isn't clear whether Welles really took in what was happening to him. He must have understood the sheer fact of the matter – he may have been a strange impetuous genius but he wasn't *that* strange. But it isn't clear whether he understood the possibly dangerous connection between his new contract and the fact that Schaefer wasn't keen on *The Magnificent Ambersons;* Schaefer's lack of interest might indicate that there would be a lack of support later on, and it perhaps ought to have made Welles himself hesitate before proceeding with the very special material of *The Magnificent Ambersons,* with its melancholy tone and its unusual length as originally planned. These were what Schaefer was uneasy about and therefore exactly what Welles could protect only by the right to final cut. Yet Welles wasn't deterred and doesn't even seem to have been warned by Schaefer's attitude.

From *Citizen Kane* and *The Magnificent Ambersons* on, Welles's relations to movie studios were never easy, when there were any relations at all. Hollywood has often been thought to be unfriendly to independent artists and unaccustomed to dealing with them, but in fact the studios housed many independent and difficult people who needed a lot of expert handling and who got it. Welles could have become one of these. On the other hand, many independent artists before and after him left Hollywood in disgust; the constraints on serious moviemaking in this commercial town were quite as powerful as they are famous. But if the studio people had learned how to handle him, and he how to handle them, he would have been the gainer, for he would have been able to use Hollywood's unrivaled technical resources to get his films made and marketed with maximum technological and commercial know-how.

When Welles returned on August 22, 1942, from a seven-month stint in Brazil – his contribution to the war effort in the form of an (eventually aborted) film project, sponsored by Roosevelt's Office of Inter-American Affairs, concerned to win South American goodwill – *The Magnificent Ambersons* had already opened, with hardly any publicity, a situation possibly even intended by the studio to evoke the indifferent response from the public that it was getting. Despite this disappointment, or to dispel it, Welles embarked on a large number of projects, few of them connected with film. He seems not to have been sure what career he was going to choose or what kind of person he was going to become. But his interest in radio had been ongoing and it remained. Five months after the release of *Citizen Kane,* he had started to write, direct, produce and host a variety show for CBS called *The Orson Welles Show,* and he continued this enterprise under different titles after his Latin American venture: as *Orson Welles Almanac* in 1944, and as *This Is My Best* in 1945. There was a lecture tour in January 1944, entitled "The Nature of the Enemy," on the subject of fascism. The role of film director doesn't seem paramount among the options he was exploring, but it began to seem that the role of politician might be. He began setting out his views about world politics on radio in *Orson Welles Commentaries* in 1945. In 1945 he also started a daily column of mainly political opinion for *The New York Post,* called first *Orson Welles Almanac* and later *Orson Welles Today.* He seemed to be testing himself in the role of politician. Welles's tremendous admiration for Roosevelt led him to work hard for him in the 1944 campaign; a brief personal contact with Roosevelt had surely made him feel the excitement of being close to power. But he also associated with people far to the left of Roosevelt, popular front pro-Soviet activists such as Lillian Hellman, a fact that would imply dangerous political naïveté but for the fact that in this respect most liberals of the time were also naïve.

Despite these serious preoccupations, one senses also a certain unrooted restlessness; but it was not unfruitful, as one sees most clearly and entertainingly in his own highly personalized version of a USO show, a populist magic act called *The Mercury Wonder Show,* which took place in "The Mercury Wonder Show Tent," on Cahuenga Boulevard in Hollywood, from August 3 until well into September in 1943 – and got good audiences.

During this period he began what became the lifelong practice of acting in films directed by others. Before he went to Latin America he had played the lead, Colonel Haki, in *Journey into Fear,* a botched creation of his own contriving, conceived and written by himself but directed by Norman Foster. In December 1943 he took on the more serious assignment of playing Rochester opposite Joan Fontaine's Jane in Robert Stevenson's *Jane Eyre.* In 1946 he costarred with Claudette Colbert in Irving Pichel's *Tomorrow Is Forever.* In 1949 he made his most famous guest appearance, as Harry Lime in Carol Reed's *The Third Man,* a role with which he became identified throughout the world. (In March 1951 he began *The Adventures of Harry Lime,* a half-hour show on BBC, lasting for thirty-nine episodes, most of which he wrote himself.) In December 1949 he appeared as Cesare Borgia in Henry King's *Prince of Foxes,* and in 1950 he played a Mogol lord in Henry Hathaway's *The Black Rose.* Much later, in 1959, he gave his ripest performance outside his own films as the Clarence Darrow figure in Richard Fleischer's film about the Leopold–Loeb murder trial, *Compulsion.*

He had returned to the theater immediately after completing the shooting of *Citizen Kane* in 1941, to produce and direct on Broadway a dramatization of Richard Wright's *Native Son.* And he returned again in 1946 on a heroic scale, with *Around the World in Eighty Days,* a large-scale venture into nondramatic, nonnarrative total theater, with songs by Cole Porter. All accounts make it sound attractive, and it almost got off

Welles at Columbus Circle, New York, in 1938, addressing the American League for Peace and Democracy. (Photo courtesy of Photofest)

the ground, but it finally didn't come together, either artistically or logistically – a failure disappointing both in itself and because it happened while Welles was losing the chance to direct Bertolt Brecht's *Galileo*. He is reported to have become interested in Brecht's alienation effect (though it isn't clear exactly how deep that interest was), and Brecht, in exile in the United States, had pleased him by coming backstage during the tryouts for *Around the World* to tell him that his show was the best thing he had seen in the theater since he had come to America. Perhaps because of some promise Brecht made, Welles came to believe he had an understanding with Brecht and Charles Laughton that he was to direct the first

American production of *Galileo,* and he also believed they had agreed that the production would wait until *Around the World* got launched. But Laughton and Brecht not only didn't wait; they awarded the production of *Galileo* to producer Mike Todd, who had made himself a permanent enemy of Welles's by having withdrawn financial backing from *Around the World* at a crucial moment. As with so many events in Welles's career, it isn't clear whether it was through his mismanagement, or Laughton's, or Brecht's, or through some unconscious stroke of rude or thoughtless behavior that he lost *Galileo;* the loss really mattered to him. In any event, he was probably well out of collaboration with the dangerously unreliable Brecht.

On the set of *Jane Eyre* Welles caught the eye of a producer, William Goetz, who promised to produce a Welles film when he put together an outfit of his own. When Goetz founded International Pictures, he came through on the promise and made it possible for Welles to make *The Stranger* in 1946. Welles made it known generally that he planned in this new film to avoid excess and to produce a conventional Hollywood work, moderate, uneccentric. and middle-of-the-road in mood and technique. And he did achieve this, while exploiting his gift for workmanlike dramatic construction. *The Stranger,* about a Nazi hiding out in a college town in New England, is not ineffective in its mode, though not very interesting. When he began shooting *The Lady from Shanghai,* in 1946, he compensated for the moderation of *The Stranger* by technical dazzle and perverse moodiness of tone. *The Lady from Shanghai* looked promising commercially, since it featured the superstar Rita Hayworth, who was married to Welles when the film was planned. But despite Hayworth's popularity as the reigning Hollywood love-goddess, and despite the vogue for film noir, that then-yet-unnamed category in which many have placed *The Lady from Shanghai*, Welles's tone and technique seem to have been too puzzling and abstruse to win the success he had planned and hoped for – many people still can't figure out exactly what happens in the twisted plot line. Among the already sizable audience of Welles enthusiasts, though, the brilliant film was welcomed with excitement.

Although *The Lady from Shanghai* did not obtain general release until 1948, it had been completed in 1947. Immediately afterward Welles received a proposal about directing for the theater, which was to reactivate his imagination, his energy and his genius. He initially had to turn it down because he was tentatively committed to an arrangement with Alexander Korda, the British producer, to film Wilde's *Salomé;* Korda reneged at the last minute, claiming to be out of money, as he was to do again later in

Welles's career. Temporarily without a project, Welles reconsidered the offer he had turned down, an unusual one from an outfit called the American National Theater and Academy (ANTA) in New York; the offer was to direct something, anything, at the Utah Centennial Festival in Salt Lake City. Welles accepted; *King Lear* was his first idea, but in the end he chose the play with which he had had his first success in New York, *Macbeth*.

As he began to think about the project, his ultimate goal became making a film of *Macbeth*, and he welcomed the chance to stage it in Utah mainly as an opportunity for longer and deeper rehearsal for the film. Studio backing for a Shakespearean venture would in the past have been close to impossible to get, but the great success in the United States of Laurence Olivier's *Henry V* in 1946 had changed this, and Welles was able to get backing before leaving for Utah. He located the money at an unlikely place, Republic Pictures, the home of the cowboy movies of Roy Rogers and Gene Autry. Welles claimed that affiliation with this unpretentious studio was just what he wanted for a project that he always referred to as an exceptionally modest one. He planned to make *Macbeth* on a small scale, with minimal sets, costumes, and apparatus, and very rapidly, to show his professional competence and his realism; as it happened he used an almost entirely new cast. The financial guarantee may have contributed to the unusually high spirits with which he carried through the project. The stage performance of *Macbeth* opened in Salt Lake City on May 28, 1947, and ran four days; the shooting in Hollywood began June 23 and ended July 17, after only twenty-one days of actual shooting – he had achieved the record to which he had aspired.

Only the final editing of the film remained to be done. But instead of setting to work on the editing, Welles suddenly left for Europe and busied himself with other film projects there, involving Alexander Korda again – *Cyrano* and *Around the World in Eighty Days* – while the mystified and then furious businessmen at Republic tried to get him back to finish the job he had been hired for. In the end, part of the *Macbeth* footage was sent to him in Rome for editing, and he came back to Hollywood to edit another part, but much of the work was done by his associate producer, Richard Wilson. The project he had started in order to clear his name of the stain of undependability ended up confirming it more strongly. Perhaps that was what he wanted – his sudden decision to quit Hollywood may have been a kind of manifesto of rebellion against an environment he was about to leave.

These three films of the late forties – *The Stranger, Macbeth,* and *The Lady from Shanghai* – differ in tone and style, and in their personal meaningfulness to Welles, but they were all made under studio auspices, and that connection is clearly visible. Welles had experienced at RKO the studio world's capacity to damage his work, and there is no puzzle about his, or any artist's, wishing to escape the bottom-line mind-set of the system. But the studio as an institution also had the effect of centering Welles's energies and saving him from distraction; it seemed to generate the intense energy and concentration in which he had produced his great successes on Broadway, whereas the conditions of freelance, independent filming in which he was to spend the rest of his career rarely generated this productive state, if they didn't actually inhibit it. He worked in the studio atmosphere only once again in his career, in 1956, when he was settled in Hollywood for a short stay. Universal offered him a role in a thriller, *Badge of Evil,* and Charlton Heston – a great admirer of Welles, who had been offered the starring role – had the clout to engineer Welles's being asked to direct the film as well as acting in it. This was to become *Touch of Evil.* Everything about this brilliant film, including the efficiency with which it was made, shows how productively Welles could in fact work in the Hollywood studio environment.

The studio also offered the unmatchable advantage of working with the supremely skillful professional technicians of Hollywood, with whom he had always worked with pleasure and who seem to have had pleasure working with him. The loss of this resource after the forties made a difference that can be spotted at once in the "look" of all his future movies. Another loss was impending, that of his Mercury players, with their special blend of high professional skill and deep emotional relation to Welles himself. Everett Sloane, Erskine Sanford, and Gus Schilling appear in *The Lady from Shanghai,* but none of the Mercury players are in *The Stranger,* and of course none of them followed Welles on the travels that began after *The Lady from Shanghai* – not even as far as Utah for the preliminary stage version of *Macbeth.* From 1947 until April of 1956, Welles lived mainly in Europe, where his Mercury players could not have been expected to accompany him. He did work with Joseph Cotten on *The Third Man* but on an entirely different basis.

While in Europe he fashioned a dramatization of *Moby-Dick* early in 1955, which he staged in London from June 18 to July 9. He decided not to bring it to the United States, choosing *King Lear* instead; a week before the play opened he broke his ankle during a preview, and he continued the run of twenty-one performances in a wheelchair. While in America he accepted various offers ranging through the whole spectrum of show business: a magic show at the Riviera Hotel in Las Vegas, a TV version of *Twentieth Century* (opposite Betty Grable), and various programs for Desilu Productions, including the *I Love Lucy* episode "Lucy Meets Orson Welles." Welles's immersion in American show business culminated in his work on *Touch of Evil* in 1957. After that he immediately went back to Europe again, and during the next twenty years he returned to Hollywood only for brief periods, coming back permanently only in 1979, in order to be near the work that was keeping him alive: TV commercials and voice-overs.

After Hollywood, his subjects seem to have been developed in a different process from what had produced *Citizen Kane* and *The Magnificent Ambersons*. His style was always recognizable, but the array of subjects he chose don't form a clear profile of interests or personal identity. Even the selection of the Shakespeare films seems random. He made one great Shakespeare film, *Chimes at Midnight*, and two near-great ones, *Macbeth* and *Othello;* but when one compares even these rich works with *Citizen Kane* and *The Magnificent Ambersons* one notices a slight weakening of motivation and a slight loss of depth and breadth. *Citizen Kane* came out of a widely ranging and sharply motivated search for a subject, which was conducted in collaboration with a major talent, Mankiewicz, who was capable of working on Welles's level; despite the difference in temperament between him and Welles, and perhaps sometimes because of the difference, he played a large role in developing the film. We would sense the complexity of events and personalities behind the making of *Citizen Kane* even if we didn't actually know what happened. Welles wrote the screenplay for *The Magnificent Ambersons* without collaboration, but the subject came from deep within him, from his Midwestern background and his early reading; it had been long meditated and imagined, and it was about a way of life on which he was an expert.

The density and multifaceted richness of these early films come from the fact that greater creative pressure was at work in choosing a subject, with more intricate interests at stake, than in the later films. In Welles's Shakespearean subjects, where there is less of that pressure, one surmises, not to put too fine a point on it, that a different motive was at work, that of emphasizing Welles the actor. And he may have indulged that motive at a considerable cost to the free imagination and the access to complex thoughts and feelings on the part of the other Welles, the director. Nor was Welles quite the Shakespearean actor he thought he was. He had a superb voice with a unique timbre, and he was an eloquent rhetorician, marvelous at projecting extreme states of mind; but his verse reading was fairly rudimentary, and he seems never to have thought of taking hints about the movement and lineation of blank verse from listening to Olivier, Gielgud, and his other great English contemporaries. For all the boldness of their imagery, there is something conservative and two-dimensional in the Shakespeare films compared with the three-dimensional depth and inventiveness of *Citizen Kane* and *The Magnificent Ambersons*. The subject matter of the never-exhibited *The Other Side of the Wind*, with its head-on approach to autobiographical material, may have seemed to Welles a move toward greater freedom of invention; but as far as we can make it out, that material didn't actually prove productive of much free play of imagination or much complexity.

Nevertheless, whatever his limitations as a Shakespearean, Welles's Macbeth had been confident, powerful, lithe, and focused, and he was in other respects at the peak of his powers when he began shooting *Othello* on June 19, 1949, in Mogador, Morocco. The search for backers having failed, Welles decided to finance the film himself, but financial troubles began almost immediately and continued throughout the celebrated four years it took to make the film. The way *Othello* was made, indeed, forms the pattern of Welles's procedures and experiences from this point on until he gave up filmmaking in the late seventies. In the course of making the film, he was subject to cycles of activity and inactivity over which he had almost no control. Once the projected film was written, scheduled, and cast, shooting had to wait while Welles gathered the money necessary to begin (usually from acting jobs in other films, not often of high caliber); once actual shooting began, it had to be discontinued when the money ran out – as of course it always did, very quickly. Then Welles hunted for money again; but when it became available, the actors now often weren't available, and shooting had to wait until they were free from their commitments – and the cycle started up again. This paradigm of irregularity, which seems inevitable in the financial circumstances under which Welles was working, but which was widely publicized as almost a professional scandal, may have done more than anything else to establish his reputation as an artist who couldn't finish anything.

Leaving the Hollywood studio system had released him from control by the box-office criteria of the businessmen who ran Hollywood, but not of course from the necessity of finding money to back his independent film projects. And it was while making *Othello* that Welles began to live in the world he was to inhabit for the rest of his life, a world of extreme economic and social contingency, almost of squalor, in which he was humiliatingly dependent on the caprices of rich and extremely capricious men.

When they weren't very rich, they were often dishonest; when they really were very rich, they behaved with the ugly carelessness of the rich that Fitzgerald writes about in *The Great Gatsby.* Welles cultivated the habitués of this demimonde of finance because he thought there was nowhere else to go to find the money he needed; he may have been right, and in any case, whether there were better, more dependable, more dignified sources is now unknowable. A more painful possibility is that this world really pleased and satisfied something in Welles's nature. It's not only that he ate in the best restaurants and stayed in the best hotels, but that he lived in triumph in this luxury, which may have been designed as a trap for his prey but surely also fed his own sybaritic longings.

Meanwhile, like a gull in Ben Jonson or Molière, he was repeatedly disappointed, deceived, and defrauded by the men he courted, by dubious small-time denizens of the shoals of the money world, who thought they fancied a fling at the movies, and he was defrauded even by men of supposedly serious stature, such as Alexander Korda, whose high standing in the profession didn't keep him from breaking promises repeatedly, with a charm that seems always to have placated Welles. Apart from the joking anecdotes he liked to tell, we don't know what Welles felt like, living and thinking and working in this atmosphere; he was Orson Welles, so he must have prided himself on not being a whiner, on taking things in stride. A genial acceptance of whatever life offered gradually became his regular style. The rich sunniness and warmth of his manner as it appears in the Bogdanovich book[8] and in many other interviews, and in the clips from TV appearances that survive in documentaries, represent a marvelous deployment of will and energy and self; one can't help admiring, even loving, so steady a projection of sheer niceness. But what he achieved by this new self-performance isn't quite so clear: Was it courage or denial, self-performance or self-deception? This persona was what potential backers saw and were charmed by – a superb example of Welles's performing self, as he maneuvered through the corrupt world of movie financing, not with the vulgar whining of a petitioner but with the aristocratic self-delight of a performer.

The making of *Othello* has become famous for its entertaining stories of last-minute improvisations: shooting the first scene in a steam bath because the costumes hadn't arrived, or kneeling in a melodramatic plea for money before Darryl Zanuck in a hotel lobby. When Fellini filmed his send-up of this incident in *8½*, he took all the pain out of it by recasting the unflappably gracious producer from the pained, angry, and embarrassed Zanuck to an easygoing Italian vulgarian, complicit with his director's performance and getting a kick out of his self-abasement. But of course it's possible that Welles himself put on his show with just as much ironic self-command and without feeling any particular pain.

Welles's search for money took a different form in August 1950, after he had finished most of the shooting of *Othello* but had not yet begun the editing. He conceived the idea of another total-theater extravaganza, *An Evening with Orson Welles,* which he performed in leading German cities. The program included excerpts from *Doctor Faustus, The Importance of Being Earnest,* and *Henry VI;* a song recital by Eartha Kitt; and a magic show by Welles. The show got a rapturous acceptance, and a fair amount of money was made by this amusing and harmlessly relaxing diversion. But for reasons hard to make out, this venture was in some quarters interpreted as a sign of Welles's final disintegration – the executive secretary of ANTA, the outfit that had sponsored the Utah *Macbeth,* thought Welles suddenly a "lost cause" who needed a "keeper."[9] But this was a functionary of the "legitimate" theater speaking, who may well have wanted a more conventionally ordered career for Welles. One remembers that Brecht called Welles's earlier "illegitimate" endeavor the best American theater he had seen.

In his new circumstances, his new life, his new world, moving about Europe ceaselessly in search of funds and of locales for shooting, Welles made, in addition to *Othello* (1952; New York premiere, 1955), three other large-scale films: *Mr. Arkadin* in 1955, *The Trial* in 1962, and *Chimes at Midnight* in 1966. A short adaptation of an Isak Dinesen story, *The Immortal Story,* appeared in 1968, and the essay-film *F for Fake* was completed in 1973. Several films were never completed. Much time was spent on a *Don Quixote* before it was abandoned. *The Deep* was entered into as a possible commercial success, but early in the shooting the death of the leading man, Laurence Harvey, brought the hope and the proceedings to a halt, never to be resumed. In his last fifteen years Welles worked intermittently but with steady commitment on *The Other Side of the Wind,* an ambitious semiautobiographical film, starring John Huston, always on the verge of completion but again and again blocked by technical or legal difficulties. This was a project much in his thoughts, and he expected great things from it – nothing less than the retrieval of his reputation. All of these films since *Othello* were made in Europe under the same improvisatory conditions; only *Touch of Evil* was made in Hollywood, under studio conditions.

The process by which Welles financed his films often began with a casual, chance encounter with somebody who expressed an interest in getting into moviemaking. This unwary and imprudent confession would be followed by Welles's wooing and winning of this potential backer, in what must have been the most eloquent persuasion available in the Western world. Valuable energy must have gone into this often repeated process. When the money thus acquired ran out, as it soon did – for Welles never consulted a budget and never even drew one up in the first place – Welles himself then took on the task of securing more money, usually by taking acting jobs in other films. The financing of *Mr. Arkadin* (premiered in Madrid in 1955 but not opened in New York until 1962) followed a simpler structure, which drew on a personal and political tie formed earlier in Welles's life; this ought to have made the process of making the film smoother but seems to have had the opposite effect.

The film itself is a notorious shambles, and the conditions of its financial backing may offer some explanation why. The subject comes from a radio play Welles had worked up during the *Harry Lime* days: Mr. Arkadin, rich and powerful, an amnesiac who doesn't know who he is or where he came from, hires a private investigator to track down all the people who played a part in his past. His supposed motive for the investigation is to find out his identity, and to present a clear name and past to his beloved daughter; but his motive becomes ambiguous, to say the least, as each of the people the investigator turns up is murdered. Things, of course, do not end well. In the film of this rather attractive story, the juvenile leads (Robert Arden as Guy Van Stratten, the investigator, and Paola Mori, soon to become Welles's third wife, as the daughter) lack plausibility, professional ease, and know-how – everything they ought to have. Welles plays Arkadin in rather charming makeup suitable for a comic devil in a costume ball, but his amusing performance doesn't even begin to do the necessary job of making the film hold together and gather power by creating a powerful personage and making one understand the world he controls. Welles called in old friends and acquaintances – Michael Redgrave, Katina Paxinou, Mischa Auer, and Akim Tamiroff – to play characters whom Van Stratten interviews in his search for Arkadin's past, and while their superb talents are not wasted in their splendid little vignettes, they cannot organize the film into coherence all by themselves, and their performances remain separate "numbers." The cinematography, the look of the film, is the worst disappointment – raw, coarse, sloppy, dreary, its unsettling changes of texture reflecting the erratic pattern of shooting and cutting.

The chief backer and producer of this film that was to turn out so badly was Louis Dolivet, a friend and intimate collaborator of Welles's from the war days, whose warm relation with Welles had then been a mixture of personal friendship, professional admiration, and political alliance. Dolivet was a rich man (by virtue of his marriage with the actress Beatrice Straight, who played Goneril to Welles's Lear on TV), and in the forties he put a considerable amount of his own money into his chief and abiding political interest, the advocacy of world cooperation after the war; he founded an organization called Free World and a magazine with the same name, to which Welles contributed. This was the period during which Welles was seriously considering entering politics, and Dolivet was his mentor. But ten years later, in 1954, when Dolivet reappeared in Welles's life as the patron of *Mr. Arkadin,* his reaction to Welles's methods was unexpected astonishment, which turned rapidly into disgust, all this despite the fact that Welles's work habits and especially his difficulty in completing films on schedule were hardly unknown, and that Dolivet could not have been ignorant of them when he took on the assignment of backer. In any case, he was provoked virtually to fury, and since he was a man with a certain strength of will, he took the film out of Welles's hands and entrusted the editing entirely to others, with results damaging to Welles's conception. Welles had planned and shot a complex nonlinear structure, very much in the Wellesian mode, but Dolivet ordered the film recut as a straightforward linear structure, supposedly to make it more easily understood. There are rival versions of *Mr. Arkadin* now in circulation, some claiming to have restored Welles's nonlinear structure, but none is convincing.

The most lurid of Welles's ongoing financial dramas, about the making of *The Other Side of the Wind* from 1971 to 1976, has many acts and many locales, a cast of characters worthy of an international thriller, and innumerable intertwined displays of folly and deceit. More than any other single episode in Welles's life it tempts one to believe in his fatal bad luck.

He has shot almost two hours of this film in America when the intrigue begins. Welles himself, with Oja Kodar, his then-companion, has put up some $700,000, but more backing is needed. Now two other backers appear, a nameless Spaniard and the brother-in-law of the Shah of Iran. An agreement is struck to finance the film in a three-sided operation, and Welles leaves enthusiastically to resume shooting in Spain. The plan is that the Spaniard will receive money from the Iranian, which he will then forward to Welles in Spain. No money arrives, and when he is asked, the Spaniard claims he has received none from the Iranian. It emerges eventually that the Iranian has in fact given the Spaniard money as arranged, which the Spaniard has himself pocketed. In the end no legal action seems possible, Welles and Kadar lose their money, and shooting ceases. Suddenly it is learned that Welles will receive the third annual Life Achievement Award from the American Film Institute in a big ceremony in Hollywood. This happy event, along with other promising auguries, convinces Welles that he will now find Hollywood backing for *The Other Side of the Wind*, and he leads a multinational and multicultural caravan of the film's backers to the ceremony. And it turns out that one Hollywood money man, perhaps inspired by Welles's adroitly reverential and ironic speech at the convention, does make a handsome offer. But when this offer is relayed to the three-part company, named L'Astrophore, it is promptly rejected via the office of the French director of the company, Dominique Antoine, on the assumption that an even better offer would come. None ever does, and in the denouement of the drama, the Shah's death and the coming to power of Khomeini lead to the Shah's brother-in-law's being stripped of all authority over the film, which is handed over to a tough businessman of the new regime with no interest in the arts. Welles loses all the money he had invested, and he almost loses the negative to the film itself.

This was the world in which he lived and tried to work.

Welles died before this legal confusion was resolved, so that this last film, reportedly completed, has never been exhibited. But the glimpses that have been granted of its much contested footage – most notably in a recent German documentary – are depressing. Far from seeming deep or adventurous, or far out, this footage seems routine in content, and it is made with a technical ineptitude painful to contemplate as the work of the great master of technical know-how. Welles seems never to have developed competence in color photography. He was a black-and-white man, and at his best he was the best of them all; but color is something else, and the lusterless, muddy, ill-organized palette in this footage of *The Other Side of the Wind* (also in *The Deep*) hints at the possibility that he had become unaware of his own technical incapacity.

The differing circumstances surrounding the making of *Chimes at Midnight* as compared with those of *The Trial* go some way to explaining the clarity and direct humanity of Welles's final movie performance, as Falstaff, and the pretentious hollowness of his Kafka production. When the Salkinds – ubiquitous father and son, impresarios whom Welles had earlier encountered as an actor – told him they were interested in backing one of his films, they handed him a list of works in the public domain from which to choose; he chose the Kafka novel because it was the only one he could "conceive" of directing. This doesn't suggest strong motivation or much inwardness with the material. Nor does the celebrated discovery of the abandoned Gare d'Orsay in Paris and the decision to shoot the film there suggest that Welles understood the novel very intimately, since nothing could be further from the subtle understatement of Kafka's monochromatic atmosphere than this melodramatic, echoing, haunted building: Welles's use of it seems a throwback to the most passé expressionism. The gallant players can do nothing to counteract all this falsity.

Chimes at Midnight, by contrast, offers Welles in the least mannered performance of his career. He seems to have wanted to be the Falstaff we all see in our imagination, and his line reading is deliberately unidiosyncratic. The impersonation of age is straightforward. When *Chimes at Midnight* was being made Welles himself was only about fifty, yet something in his relation to the material makes it seem that he isn't impersonating age but understanding it from the inside, without his usual glow of theatricality, without seeming to be Welles the performer of Welles. He had been thinking about and acting out old age practically from the beginning of his career, from his performance as the Ghost in *Hamlet* at the Gate Theatre when he was sixteen. Again and again in *Citizen Kane* you see the young and vigorous Welles imagining what it's like to be old, imagining what *he* would be like when he got old. He has some wonderful ideas, particularly of Kane as middle-aged. The only faltering is in his makeup and sometimes his way of moving as the very old Kane. Pauline Kael gets it right: "something went blank in the aging process – not just because the makeup was erratic – but because the character lost his connection with business and politics and became a fancy theatrical notion, an Expressionist puppet."[10]

Yet there are moments when Welles is not impersonating Kane so much as inhabiting him, as he later seems to have inhabited Falstaff. This is nowhere more interesting than in the passage toward the end where Kane is not dominating Susan or tearing her room apart or being a man of will, but busying himself at Xanadu in another way – he is walking briskly downstairs, almost bouncing (Susan is at one of her puzzles over to the side), and he is totally focused and confident. And it is perfectly clear that he is *doing nothing.* The mood is sunny and cheerful, with no sense of emptiness, no looking backward; it's a benign way of looking at old age, and a kind of prediction of how Welles himself was to spend many of his days after *Chimes at Midnight.*

"The least mannered performance of his career": Welles as Falstaff in *Chimes at Midnight.* (Photo courtesy of Photofest)

2

Citizen Kane

When the head of RKO, George J. Schaefer, brought the twenty-four-year-old Orson Welles to Hollywood in 1940, he couldn't have known exactly what to expect from him, but that was the point of the invitation. Welles was the boy genius of Broadway and radio, and his speciality was the unexpected. *Citizen Kane* proved to be, as desired, different from what anybody could have predicted. The subject – the portrait of an American press lord – sailed closer to the wind than was customary in Hollywood. In caricaturing William Randolph Hearst, even in part, Welles risked offending, and in fact did offend, a power greatly feared in Hollywood, for Hearst controlled a large body of American opinion through his chain of newspapers, and therefore would exert a powerful influence on theater attendance. Surprising too – though perhaps not so surprising, since Welles was in the process of inventing it as he worked with his great cinematographer, Gregg Toland – was the high cinematic style of *Citizen Kane,* with its manifold visual tricks and devices, its far from unobtrusive artifice, its extreme chiaroscuro, its constantly self-delighting brilliance. 'It's just one big special effect,' detractors might well have complained: 'a character can't even walk down a hall in his own house in this movie without being reflected in a hundred mirrors.' But the rich style of *Citizen Kane* was a language that could be used well or badly, and in this first film Welles used it with the flexibility, depth, and intelligence of a master. He could even command the virtuosity to use it playfully.

A more riskily unexpected element in *Citizen Kane* was its narrative method. Welles and his brilliant colleague, Herman J. Mankiewicz, invented a structure new to Hollywood and unfamiliar in dramatic and cinematic art in general, which replaced ordinary linear narrative with a sort of dialectic between different perspectives, in which all the elements of the film – the story, the characters, the general mood, our understanding of it all – advance by means of an argument between opposites. The unexpected miracle was that this tricky, fancy, gimmicky film turned out to have real emotional weight and insight into human predicaments. It has also had great staying power; *Citizen Kane* has repeatedly taken first place in the *Sight and Sound* polls of the greatest movies of all time. For almost everybody, Welles's artificial style has come to seem natural and central to this film, and a great kind of moviemaking.

A stylistic device that Welles uses repeatedly, especially in making transitions, is connected with the art of magic, an art dear to his heart. When he was doing magic he is said to have been at his most natural, spontaneous and playful, and he considered himself with some justification to have nearly professional standing in the field. And the echoes of magic in *Citizen Kane* point to an essential characteristic of Welles's art. Like magic, his cinema is an art of performance, in which the artist displays and performs his skill and virtuosity – his bag of tricks – directly to and for the admiration and applause of an audience, an art that, if it is working in the dramatic medium of cinema, presents the phenomenon of dramatic illusion as a creation of virtuosity as well as an instrument for making dramatic effects and meanings. This was to remain Welles's essential art, but in *Citizen Kane* he extended it enormously to develop a wide range of expression – of meaning, feeling, and tone – and to move his audience not only to admiration and applause but to sympathetic engagement.

Early in the film, while rich young Charlie Kane is trying, for "fun," to run a sad little newspaper called *The Inquirer,* he takes his two closest colleagues, Leland (Joseph Cotten) and Bernstein (Everett Sloane), to look at a photograph of the staff of a rival paper, *The Chronicle. The Inquirer* is doing badly, in circulation and otherwise, despite attempts at yellow journalism (there's a takeoff on Hearst's rumored role in fomenting the Spanish–American War), but *The Chronicle* always does well, as you can tell from the air of complacent power and prestige in the photograph of the staff. While the three young men are looking at the photograph in the window of *The Chronicle,* the camera moves in closer to it, as if to study it more carefully; then, unexpectedly, Kane himself, who we assumed was still looking in the window and talking with his friends, appears in an entirely different perspective, walking smilingly toward us in front of the photograph, which seems to have become life-size – for a moment we think somebody has made a gigantic enlargement of it. A moment later, we see that it isn't a photograph at all; and then the whole thing clicks into focus and we catch on to the trick that fooled us. We laugh and feel like applauding – applauding Kane, who brought off the trick, and behind him, Welles, who dreamed it up and brought it off too. The photograph was brought to life in Charlie Kane's special style – he envied the power and prestige of *The Chronicle*, so he simply bought its entire staff for his own paper. Now he's bragging about his coup by having these men photographed again, in the same formation as before, but as the staff of *The Inquirer,* as *his* staff; and he orders the new photograph sent to *The Chronicle* as a taunt.

Charlie's trick might seem callow and sophomoric, but it actually doesn't as we experience it. Whatever our misgivings about Kane's egotism, his arrogance, his need to get what he wants and his way of getting it, they melt away into the pleasure we take in the performance he is putting on in front of us, a performance into which Orson Welles, the young actor who is playing Kane, is also pouring his own charm and charisma. Earlier Charlie had scandalized Walter Parks Thatcher (George Coulouris), the Wall Street trustee of his estate (a man easily scandalized), by writing in a letter from abroad, "I think it would be fun to run a newspaper." He was kidding Thatcher, but in fact it was a pretty accurate account of his way of going about things, as the scene with the photograph of the *Chronicle* staff testifies. And if he uses his money to buy people as well as newspapers, this doesn't come through as a big moral issue; the *Chronicle* staff he bought was apparently buyable, and in any case we don't take that staff quite seriously as human beings – they aren't much more substantial in Charlie's magic act than the rabbits he might have pulled out of a hat in a different act. Transforming the classically unethical act of treating people like things into playfulness and wit is part of the fun he told Thatcher he was anticipating.

Kane himself offers another image: "Six years ago I looked at a picture of the world's greatest newspapermen. I felt like a kid in front of a candy store. Well, tonight, six years later, I got my candy, all of it." Nothing wrong with buying candy in a candy store – that's why it's there. Charlie is finessing all issues of moral compunction, and we join him when we enjoy watching the trick and being fooled by it. It somehow makes it better that he seems to know exactly what he's doing, as we realize when he decorates his message with playful irony, with witty words and sardonic glances. Watching Kane's gaiety turn willfulness into a self-delighting performance of his own nature becomes a tribute to transformation, metamorphosis, and change, and to the energy that makes transformation an act of life. And in 1940 there was an additional pleasure in recognizing

The "fun" of running a newspaper: the young Kane (Welles) – with his friends, Jedediah Leland (Joseph Cotten) at left, and Bernstein (Everett Sloane) – holding his Statement of Principles, drawn up for the morning edition. (Photo courtesy of Photofest)

that Kane's words were spoken by a voice already known to us and famous throughout America: the voice of Orson Welles on the radio.

At a later party for Kane, his friend Jedediah Leland tries to raise those ethical issues with Bernstein, Kane's loyal manager, but the magic of Kane's performance has already dissolved the issues, and Leland's fussing seems comically dismal and obtuse. More interesting things are taking place at the big party Kane is giving to celebrate his own and *The Inquirer*'s triumph, with dancing girls and a made-to-order musical tribute to Kane as a fighting liberal, sung by a leading vaudeville song-and-dance man. With all this going on, it is hard to hear even the sound of Leland's scruples. While Leland and Bernstein are trying to talk, we are watching the background, catching the spectacle of Charlie dancing with the showgirls – or trying to dance, in a temporary lapse in self-assurance, for his awkward, embarrassed movements show that he isn't having fun so much as making himself have fun, and in a medium in which he is far from being a master. The song toasts Kane as a man of liberal ideals, but Leland is wondering whether Kane's liberalism will last: Won't the staff he has bought away from *The Chronicle* go on writing the yellow journalism they used to write? But Bernstein's proud belief in Kane never falters – "he'll have them changed to his kind of newspapermen in a week." Leland keeps on fretting: "There's always a chance, of course, that they'll change Mr. Kane – without his knowing it." Though Bernstein, who enjoyed the trick with the photograph, welcomes transformation and change, Leland is worried about it; yet his worry, lacking energy to begin with, drops away from our attention in our pleasure in the show Kane and Welles are staging.

The film raises doubts rather like Leland's during other discussions of Kane's values and behavior, and disposes of them in similar ways: in a scene with Thatcher and Bernstein in 1929, for instance, when Kane is being forced to relinquish "all control" of his newspaper empire, while continuing "to maintain over [his] newspapers a large measure of control" – whatever such double-talk might mean. It is a richly inflected scene, its simple set fully evocative of the power of the financial system, and there is an interchange loaded with the sound of meaningfulness at the end: "You know, Mr. Bernstein, if I hadn't been very rich, I might have been a really great man." Thatcher asks, "What would you like to have been?" and Kane answers, "Everything you hate." This has the format of a deep exploration of Kane's nature, but it is only magic, sleight of hand – it would turn out to have a false bottom if we looked closely. But we don't look closely. We are distracted from this critical questioning by the format and the style – the powerfully terse summing-up of Kane's "Everything you hate" has a satisfactory meaning by virtue of its very shape. At the same time we are also being moved and persuaded by Welles's movingly sympathetic impersonation of the meditative middle-aged Kane, looking back over his achievements and his failures, with irony and – in an almost dreamy smile – with what looks like self-forgiveness.

Kane's magic with the photograph is the action of a character inside a movie, but it is doubled outside the movie by Welles himself, who as director of the film is performing the same trick at the same moment. Both performances imply and need an audience to achieve their full effect. Kane is making his staff an audience, and Welles is making us his audience. It is a box within a box. When we enjoy such performances and want to applaud the performer, it is good to know exactly whom to clap for, and in this case there he is, right in front of us, the actor who is impersonating a witty and glowingly self-pleased young man, and doing it to perfection because he actually is a witty and glowingly self-pleased young actor named Orson Welles, directing his first film and doing everything he can

The middle-aged Kane, with Thatcher (George Coulouris), left, and Bernstein, formally relinquishes control of his newspaper empire. "If I hadn't been very rich, I might have been a really great man." (Photo courtesy of Photofest)

think of to dazzle us with magic and the tricks of his just-acquired film technique. Rarely has there been such a consonance between a film and its maker. We like Welles's performances partly because they want so much to be liked, but that wouldn't be a virtue if they weren't so inventive and so accomplished.

When Welles first saw the equipment at RKO he is supposed to have said, "No boy was ever given a better electric train to play with," and Kane's trick with the photograph unmistakably shows us Orson Welles with that electric train. His delight in playing with the medium he so quickly mastered, his self-display as a performer, both actor and director, his pleasure in working his beloved magic into his movie style – these elements of Welles's style all hang together and create a unity that is partially responsible for the fullness and depth of feeling and meaning in *Citizen Kane*. Unity of such dimension and perfection, quickened into such life, doesn't happen often in art, and Welles never achieved it again. But his performance of self, his self-display, his fascination with tricks of style – these continued to be his method throughout his life, often to exciting and moving effect.

Welles's style of many devices may be what Pauline Kael meant when she mistakenly called *Citizen Kane* "a shallow masterpiece."[1] But his magical tricks, his extraordinary facility, were not antithetical to deep effects, and he achieved them in *Citizen Kane* and in most of his other films. He was in charge of his technique, not the other way around, and he guided it easily through a wide range of tones and emotions. Much later in the film, for instance, just after Kane has met Susan Alexander (Dorothy Comingore), who will become his mistress and his second wife, he sits listening with pleasure to her play and sing in the parlor of her boardinghouse, and this situation becomes the occasion for another of Kane and Welles's sleights of hand, this time in a different key and tone. While we are looking and listening, noting the infinite feebleness of Susan's performance and her lack of confidence, noting too that Kane doesn't notice this, something else starts to happen. Gradually her drab clothes and the drab furniture of the boardinghouse, including the parlor upright, dissolve into elegant clothes and an elegantly furnished room, with a grand piano, while Kane's upholstered chair turns into an exotic Oriental wicker affair, in which he holds benevolent court like a pasha. Susan has learned not to bang on the piano, but her singing itself has improved only minimally if at all – something we notice only out of the corner of our ear. As with the *Chronicle* staff, Kane has used his money to acquire Susan and to install her in a setting that fits her new position as his mistress, and also, more to the point, fits his own taste and dignity, his sense of himself and of his status. Revising Susan's clothes and furniture upward must have happened as smoothly as the transformation of the photograph of the newspaper staff, and this must also have been the case with the acquisition of Susan herself, brought off with effortless will and managerial skill in which Kane must have been oblivious to any opposition and all consequences – as the rest of the film painfully bears out.

What happened here might seem only the telescoped narrative of the process by which Kane helped Susan make what the papers later called their "love nest." Yet we witness the metamorphosis not with the sense that the style has taken a shortcut but with the sense that we again have been in touch with the processes of transformation and change themselves. This time Kane's magic isn't the occasion for joking – we don't think of him as being amused at what he has done, nor is the film amused, nor are we. Choosing and refashioning a mistress wouldn't be something

Susan (Dorothy Comingore), her apartment having improved more than her singing, performs for her fondest audience, Charles Foster Kane. (Photo courtesy of Photofest)

to joke about even for this man of will – perhaps especially not for him. We aren't shown Kane's reaction to this trick at all, as we were with the photograph, and this is a shift in meaning and style. Though Kane was responsible for the change, it is not Kane whom we perceive as the master of the trick of transformation, it is the magic of the film's style itself that we seem to be watching. The transformation of Susan has a different tone from the one with the photograph. We actually watch it taking place, for one thing – which is to say that we watch something important being done to somebody. So that the way Susan turns into the new Susan and the old parlor turns into the new flat doesn't simply charm us but makes us think, makes us in fact feel a bit apprehensive about what's going to happen.

Both transformations make key points about Kane's insistent desires, his drive to fulfill them, his power and efficiency in doing so, the self-satisfaction and wit with which he contemplates what he has made happen – these transformations characterize Kane. They also have a narrative function, moving the story line along with the speed and economy characteristic of transformation. And we shall see how basic the theme and the process of transformation, metamorphosis, and change are to the style of the film itself.

Another spectacular transformation immediately follows. It works with a different mode of modulation, from the *sound* of Kane applauding Susan in the changed living room, to the louder and larger applause at a Kane-for-governor rally Leland is addressing, followed by another modulation from the sound of Leland's speech about Kane's values, to the sound of that speech continued in Kane's own voice inside Madison Square Garden, in front of a huge photograph of himself. These modulations, which move with the effortless speed of all magical transformation, give us the sensation of being propelled through the story by an excitingly strong force, which we ascribe to both Kane and the style of the film itself.

The contrast between the transformation of the photograph and the device of Susan and her room marks a development in tone in the film and a development in Kane's character, in his egotism, from the youthful brio of the first newspaper days to the slow pomposity of the lost, empty man who got his clothes spattered by mud in the street and then was helped by Susan. He met Susan just when he was hunting for his past, and he instantly believes he has met in her the consolation and acceptance he lost and still yearns for – and perhaps she really could give him that; but in the end he can't keep himself from destroying the possibility. The value, even the meaning of Kane's gifts, his love, is something of a mystery throughout the film. Later Susan says, justly about Kane's offer to give her a picnic in the Everglades: "You never give me anything I really care about." But when he engineers the metamorphosis of Susan from sheet-music shopgirl to mistress, and of her setting from boardinghouse to elegant apartment, his wanting to do so and his ability to do so with power and efficiency have something to do with some kind of love.

The metamorphosis that installed Susan in her luxury apartment generates in reaction a reverse trick of metamorphosis that rebukes Kane's desire and power, another magical transformation, but with a great difference in tone. When Kane's wife Emily (Ruth Warrick) is told about Susan by Boss Jim Gettys (Ray Collins), Kane's rival in the election for governor, she forces him to accompany her to the house where Susan lives, which we have already seen – 185 West 74th Street. Waiting on the doorstep to be admitted, Kane takes by habit the role of master of the situation: "I had no idea you had this flair for melodrama, Emily," he says drily. (Even this little bit of Mankiewicz's screenplay shows the originality of wit and invention that enlivens its every word.) But Kane's confidence disintegrates and the scene explodes into a violent quarrel among Kane, Gettys, and Emily, all of them united only in ignoring Susan's plaintive, "But what about me?" Emily assumes that her position as betrayed wife warrants her taking charge and giving orders, but her cold, controlling tone makes it inconceivable that Kane would accept her suggestion, which he refuses outright, that he save appearances by returning home with her. He opts instead for the crazed hope that the voters, his "people," will remain loyal to him despite the scandal when he chooses to stay with Susan. As Gettys and Emily leave together, Kane loses all control and, shouting, careens down the staircase after them, straining his voice and every blood vessel of his body with threats to send Gettys to Sing Sing – a painfully ineffectual display not of power but of the desire for power, for we know that he has already lost the election, and probably much more.

And then, when the dramatic scene is over and all the characters have left, the film itself has something to add. The camera moves in to examine the number of the building, "185," which gradually changes into the dimmer, duller, washed-out black-and-white tones of the *photograph* of the number "185" as it appears the next day in the scandal story on the first page of *The Chronicle*. Kane has been hoist with his own petard quite exactly. The number "185" is freighted with the irony of classical tragedy, for Kane's hubris has blinded him precisely to the damage his own kind of journalism can and will do to him.

Welles must have used these transformation devices as transitions because they came naturally to him and because he enjoyed thinking them up and playing with them: 'Why don't we do one of those things again?' you can almost hear him suggest. But the originality and the genius of *Citizen Kane* lies, as "185" shows, in Welles's being able to transform the playful wit of these magical devices into deep, often painful meanings and feelings, and to mold them together to form the movie's essential and coherent style. Nobody could miss the meaning of young Kane's fun with the newspaper; but the transformation of Susan yields a darker and more disturbing meaning, for the contrast with the brio and charm of the earlier newspaper photograph brings out the thickening of Kane's willfulness. The same device can handle both tones and make the connection between them vivid and tight; *Citizen Kane* is a rich, tight, and unified work of art because this is the case.

The central device of transition by metamorphosis is also transition by contradiction, and it is writ large in *Citizen Kane* in the inner contradictions in the single huge passage that opens the film – a montage sequence organized by contrasts into a cinematic form of dialectic, which among its other effects wittily keeps us in doubt for a while about what kind of film we're seeing. At the very beginning we seem to be encountering a kind of Gothicism, as the camera moves up the dark mountain to Xanadu, past "No Trespassing" signs and forbidding chain fences, deserted golf courses and zoos, up the walls and into the windows of the huge house itself, finally reaching the solitary lighted room where Kane is dying. All is dark and menacing, yet there is a hint of playful exaggeration in the eerie solemnity. Bernard Herrmann's foreboding music adds self-mocking exaggerations and parodies of its own. Then, just as we are beginning to buy into the idea that the film is a seriocomic parody, we are electrified by something seriously upsetting – a monstrous close-up of huge lips under a bristling mustache, whispering the word that filled the theaters of the world with a sound never heard before – "Rosebud." No playfulness of tone here, but original, powerful, and disturbing invention, though not without serious wit in the astonishing dimension of the image – it's a peculiarly violent and aggressive contact with the human body. Next there is an action involving somebody lying on a bed and the breaking of a paperweight with a little snow scene inside, an obviously significant but unidentified object; finally a nurse enters to cover the body with the sheet that signifies death. The light fades, in a slow finale that seems to bring the ambiguity about tone to rest.

And then, against this quasi-religious hush, which we seem to be expected to take seriously, the screen explodes into the flash of a noisy, brightly lit *News on the March*, a parody of the style in which Henry Luce's *March of Time* film journalism might present the life of the man with whom we have just had our little contact. This newsreel does in fact give us important information about the Charles Foster Kane we have, it is now clear, just seen on his deathbed, but there is also much to entertain us in the parody: the announcer's fruity voice, so lusciously mimicked, the vulgarities of Luce-talk with its know-it-all condescension toward anything and everything. Another jolt brings us back to dramatic contrasts of light and dark, perhaps menacing, until we see that we are watching the special patterns of lights and shadows in the screening room

"I had no idea you had this flair for melodrama, Emily." Boss Gettys (Ray Collins) in the doorway at the "love nest," with Emily (Ruth Warrick) at the right. (Photo courtesy of Photofest)

in which the test run of *News on the March* has just taken place. The news film isn't right, it turns out – not personal enough. Who *was* Kane, really? – all we know is what he *did*. What about that dying word? What does "Rosebud" mean? The staff is sent out to investigate Kane's private life, a plausibly serious journalistic quest, but there's plenty of joking about the project, and the tone is set by the boss's final charge – "Rosebud, dead or alive! It will probably turn out to be a very simple thing" – delivered in moody darkness.

This dialectic of contrast gives us the basic pattern of the film's method and structure, each scene contrasting, often diametrically, with what has just preceded it. The pattern doesn't disappear from our consciousness to become the invisible language of the film; again and again it is emphasized as a special effect. In this as in a hundred other ways, we realize that we are experiencing an art in which the artist is licensed to manipulate his devices quite visibly to create his effects, instead of keeping himself hidden behind the work. Such openness is ordinarily avoided on principle by serious artists, but it is of the essence in Welles's work, as it is with all theatrical artists. His idiom is that of disobedience to the tact and discretion mandatory in most high art, and he is so far from being uneasy about making his audience conscious of his presence that he seeks every occasion to make it happen.

The nonrhetorical simplicity, clarity, and purity of style in the films of certain master directors – De Sica, for instance, or, at the level of vernacular popular cinema, Howard Hawks – who seem to want to be invisible behind their work, has set a standard that for some people brings into question the value of Welles's florid and mannered style, as it has also brought into question the style of a master like Eisenstein, and others. Distaste for a richly rhetorical style may be an intelligent and well-earned sensibility, but it may also amount to a puritanical refusal to allow art its full range. No one has ever accused Welles's flamboyance of being puritanical; but that flamboyance has for some people hidden his talent for modulation between modes, and for serious effects and serious meanings, which didn't get undercut or cheapened by his florid performing style but acquired vividness and strength from it.

The large-scale dialectic of thesis and antithesis in *Citizen Kane*, which is represented so clearly by the contradictions of the opening, is part of the whole imagery of change to which the film owes its meaning and life. *Citizen Kane* is about the great shifting vicissitudes in the career of a powerful man, and in the careers of all of us, about losing what one loves, about growing old, and it is often about the changes that take the form of contradiction and denial; its method fits its meaning, presenting in texture and structure a whole kaleidoscope of shifting and contrasting images of change. The movement of *Citizen Kane* is often agitated and restless on the surface, but a deep undercurrent of meditation gives force and body to the energy of that surface.

This energy is exhilaratingly visible in the presentation of Kane's first marriage. When Thompson asks Leland what Kane's marriage was like, he answers, "It was a marriage just like any other marriage"; but next, contradicting Leland's bored debunking prelude, the film itself offers a sequence that's not at all bored and not like anything else in the film. The disintegration of the Kane marriage is traced through six breakfast scenes that merge into each other in rapid dissolves – a structure clearly related to the magical transformations we have already seen. It is a dazzling sequence and utterly exhibitionistic – no device has ever advertised itself more openly as a device. The whole sequence is so sure of itself, so fast, so funny, and so brilliantly detailed, that we absorb the meanings it delivers almost without noticing them. But they are extremely interesting and intelligent meanings, like everything else in this dazzling film.

In the first episode we are touched as well as amused by the yearnings and hesitations of the young couple on a morning after they've stayed up all night to go to six parties. They're younger and more vulnerable than they'd seemed before – not as good-looking, either, which seems to mean something that's hard to pin down. Emily looks shy but not quite off-puttingly shy – rather tentative about her shyness, as it were; Charlie tries out a joke, pretending with a napkin on his arm to be a waiter serving his new wife, but she doesn't notice. The ways the young husband and wife express their feelings are far apart and so, probably, are the feelings themselves. Charlie's impersonation of romantic style and his sexual eagerness are in slightly disturbing tension with Emily's prim hesitation – behavior she may not exactly intend but can't help generating because her breeding orders her to. When Kane, with a clumsily executed sexy leer, invites her to leave the breakfast table to make love, the scene ends before you see her response, but it's so clear that the two are on different tracks that you can't imagine her saying yes. The mild little scene is essentially comic and affectionate, but with warnings about the future.

Five subsequent scenes at the breakfast table chronicle the deterioration of this marriage step by step – the coarsening of Kane's energy, the amplification of his willfulness, and the full flowering of Emily's taste for censorious control. The dissolves between the scenes are fast, and the character and narrative points swiftly and concisely made – the pacing is exhilarating. Kane's work at the newspaper keeps him out in the evenings, Emily complains irritably, for reasons which have mainly to do with propriety (other men of her set don't work at night), but may also hint at loneliness and even some suspicion about Kane's extramarital love life. There is strong anti-Semitism, not just the conventional, social kind, in her italicized distaste for Bernstein, Kane's manager – "Your Mr. Bernstein sent Junior the most incredible atrocity yesterday, Charles. I simply can't have it in the nursery." (Kane welcomes Bernstein's visits to the nursery.) The anti-Semitism suggests a whole range of other prejudices. Emily scolds Kane for using *The Inquirer* to attack the president of the United States (who is her "Uncle John"); when he delivers the wisecrack that her uncle's presidency is a mistake that will soon be corrected, we are hearing the first hint that he is thinking about entering politics himself. They keep on breakfasting together, out of inertia or to preserve appearances, probably, but they speak less and less, and by the last episode their warfare has become silent, cold, and without either the passion or the pleasure of open anger, with Kane at his end of the table reading *The Inquirer,* Emily at her end reading *The Chronicle.*

The sequence delivers a lot of important information, but its life as art lies in the wealth of its detail – clothes, hairdos, tableware, all boldly invented, accurately executed, interesting to look at for themselves, and full of meaning. The changes in Emily's hairdo show what the marriage is doing to her and move us strangely with their painful concreteness. We read her new cruel, tightly drawn style as subservience to fashion, but also as a half-deliberately chosen impulse to unsex herself; whatever its motive, it exerts a punishing pressure on her spirit, drying up her freshness and her femininity – the femininity in which, we presume, Kane has long lost interest.

Kane in contrast is dressed expansively, inventively, and with some splendor throughout the whole sequence, drawing on talents Welles had already fully developed on the stage. There is a photograph of him as Dr. Faustus, in 1937, wearing an extravagantly capacious floor-length cloak, a costume almost comically excessive. He is photographed from slightly below, and he may be standing on tiptoe; his head is thrown back, and he is looking up with rapture at the light in which he is bathed. There's an ecstatic abandon that would be foolish, if it weren't so winningly eager, as this young, twenty-two-year-old actor pours his body and mind into the meaning he wants that cloak to express. Welles had a knack for wearing extravagant costumes expressively throughout his career – in *Othello* and *Touch of Evil,* in *The Third Man* and *Compulsion* as well as in romantic historical clinkers like *The Black Rose* or *Prince of Foxes* or even *Jane Eyre.* It is a gift hard to name and hard or perhaps impossible to acquire, since it involves nothing less than being gifted with the body, the carriage, and the self-assurance that can make costumes legible, vivid, and meaningful; but then all acting depends entirely on one's way of carrying oneself, and success in any art involves being lucky as well as gifted. The accuracy and eloquence of the costumes in *Citizen Kane* give depth to many of its scenes – the richness of the costumes and the assurance with which they are worn adding to the density of the film's texture, which comes to represent the observation and understanding with which the subject is being presented.

Many of the costumes are deliberately extravagant, aimed directly at admiration and applause. When Kane rushes, almost hurtles, into the newspaper office to tell the staff of his engagement to Emily Norton, he

The final – and silent – breakfast-table scene: Kane is reading the *Inquirer;* Emily is reading its competitor. Note her hairdo. (Photo courtesy of Photofest)

is wearing a dazzling white Palm Beach suit: expensive, excessive, and absolutely, thrillingly right. You might think he is too big to wear such conspicuous clothes, but this is Charles Foster Kane and, behind him, Orson Welles, who can dare anything, and wear anything – and a sight to behold they are in these yards of luxurious white. Kane is flustered because of the impending marriage he is announcing, but being Kane, he is also utterly careless of the effect he is making in his grand suit, or of any conventional requirement to behave in a particular way. With like assurance he wears an elegantly bold striped robe in one of the breakfast-table scenes with Emily – a costume matching the insolence you see in his face. The dress clothes he wears to lay a foundation stone, and on which he comically spills some of the cement, are correctness itself. He makes ordinary clothes eloquent – disheveled ones like the rumpled suit and unbuttoned shirt in the showdown with Leland, or the beautifully tailored suit in which he signs away much of his financial power, a scene in which the rich Wall Street correctness of the clothes merges poignantly with his middle-aged stoutness to bear witness to the conventional, stuffy life the impetuous young man of the past has come to live.

The dynamic structure of contrast and change in *Citizen Kane* is most visible in the celebrated multiple points of view from which the story is told, an overall device that matches and holds together the multiplicity of the film's stylistic details. This structure seems to have been used first in film in Preston Sturges's script for *The Power and the Glory* (1933), another biography of a great public figure, which dazzled the executive Jesse Lasky and made Sturges famous. The Sturges–Welles connection ought to be a rich and significant chapter of movie history, since they are the only original geniuses who thrived as writer-directors in the studio system, even if only for a short time. But Welles says he never saw Sturges's film, and it is hard to make out any influence in tone or detail; and Sturges's script, despite its fame, turns out on inspection to be pretty ordinary, with no trace of Sturges's distinctive mind or voice.

The multiple perspective in *Citizen Kane* begins as the reporter, Thompson (William Alland) carries out his assignment from the *News on the March* postmortem, interviewing in succession Susan (unsuccessfully), Thatcher (in absentia – he has died), Bernstein, Leland, Susan again, and finally Raymond (Paul Stewart), Kane's butler at Xanadu. We see the beginning of each interview, then a narrative showing the actions reported by the character interviewed. The narratives keep to one point of view in the sense that they never show anything the character could not have seen, and it is implied that the narratives have higher ambitions, to represent not just the physical and visual perspective of the characters, but the way they felt about what they saw, and the way their personalities colored what they saw and were colored by it. But this aspect of the ambitious design turns out, like so much else in the film, to be largely the work of an illusionist – much of the time it is a trompe l'oeil of multiperspective structure that we encounter. Yet these illusions are always interesting and always sufficient – there is never a moment when we need or want a point of view to be fuller or different. The fluency with which the various breadths and depths of these points of view are briefly investigated and then abandoned with grace and ease is another instance of Welles's skill in modulation.

When Mankiewicz and Welles choose to make it so, the meaning and tone of a scene will seem to be controlled by the character's perspective, but when not, not. And it is most often not. After Susan's furious, hysterical refusal to be interviewed, Thompson next "interviews" the dead

The "dazzling white Palm Beach suit" – and the engagement announcement to the staff. (Photo courtesy of Photofest)

Thatcher by consulting his memoir in the inner sanctum of the Thatcher Memorial Library. Thatcher's memoir never takes anything like an attitude toward what he is reporting – that is not Thatcher's style. Nor is the design of that library itself how Thatcher would see it. Instead it is a freewheeling satire of Thatcher himself, a rude send-up of his pomposity – at once a bank vault, a mausoleum, a prison, a cathedral – and a library containing one book, Thatcher's unpublished memoir. Gigantic metal doors clang threateningly while a shaft of light streams down unctuously from a high window onto the sacred pages Thompson is grudgingly allowed to study. Bertha, the librarian, who is dressed and coiffed like the warden of a women's prison, immediately spots Thompson as a troublemaker – she can see he is bound to want to do something against the rules. Yet there is suddenly some Wellesian playfulness with this gorgon, in the cooing tones she addresses to her deliciously plump darling, Jennings, the guard – we feel privileged to get so enchanting a peek into her private life. But disrespect returns in Thompson's parting, "Thanks for the use of the hall."

The impudence of the set has no connection with the story about Kane that Thatcher's memoir tells. He was called to a Colorado mining town by the newly rich former boardinghouse proprietor, Mrs. Kane – she had unexpectedly inherited the world's third richest gold mine from a deadbeat customer long forgotten – to become by virtue of his office in his bank an overseer of her son Charlie's estate. Against the father's will – without consulting him – she has decided that her son should be raised by others, away from his home, and that Thatcher is to be his guardian. Thatcher witnesses the strained relation between Charlie's mother and father, which puts Charlie in a conflict of loyalty, but Thatcher records this without comment – we can tell from his face that he doesn't try to understand such things. He feels no impulse to notice or comment on Charlie's mother's mysterious presence and power. Agnes Moorehead's classic performance transcends the crudely motivational lines she has to speak ("That's why he's going to be brought up where you can't get at him"), passing beyond motives to make concrete actuality out of Mrs. Kane's inaccessibility. We may not clearly know what moved Kane's mother to send him away, and it may be foolish to have felt we needed to know; Moorehead's face so entirely fills the mind and imagination and the screen, and haunts us so persistently afterward, that there is no encouragement to ask questions.

It is natural that Thatcher, who is not an observant person, should fail to comment on this family scene or have any particular attitude toward it; he is an official organizing his client's financial affairs. But the film has assigned him another, oddly important narrative task, that of getting hit in the stomach by Charlie's sled and pushed into the snow. Thatcher passes through this and everything else in the scene without knowing what hit him, in any sense. After Charlie has left his home and family in company with his new guardian, we are mischievously misled by a smoothly deceptive transition on the part of the film itself. Charlie's abandoned sled remains in the yard, piling up with snow – time is passing, this conventional device reports – and we see him next getting a fancier sled from Thatcher for Christmas, which of course he doesn't like – it's not like his nice old one. The old sled, though we don't know it yet, is of course the Rosebud we are all searching for. It's witty and sad that we in the audience should be the only people paying attention to it – and we're not doing even that, for we're too far away to see its name, and what takes our attention anyway is the film cliché of snow piling up to register the passage of time. A powerful balancing rhyme with this trick is sounded in the final scene, when we are again the only people who watch the same sled

"Charlie's mother's mysterious presence and power" – reflected here in the face of her son (Buddy Swan), who is about to slam the top-hatted Thatcher with that sled. Harry Shannon, at left, is Charlie's father; Agnes Moorehead (of course) is his mother. (Photo courtesy of Photofest)

burn and see the name come into its own at last. We alone see Rosebud abandoned, and we see it twice, for all that matters. How Mankiewicz and Welles must have enjoyed playing fair with the audience in these games.

When Charlie gets the new sled at Christmas, we see Thatcher's severe figure from below, looming exaggeratedly down at him, so the scene is presented not from Thatcher's perspective but from Charlie's. In the next short episodes Thatcher repeatedly reacts with astonishment and outrage to everything Charlie does, but he doesn't of course share our comic view of his own behavior. The film isn't weakened or even much changed by never presenting things the way Thatcher sees them. Our sense that we are experiencing his perspective is maintained by keeping him physically before us, so that the whole sequence seems to remain his story. We don't really need or want his point of view – it's not hard to imagine his rigid conventionality, in any case – and its absence frees us to take the ironic attitude toward him that initiates the search for Rosebud on the desired note.

The following interview, with Bernstein, is warm with this character's uncomplicated friendliness, mirrored in turn in the hopefulness and cheerfulness of his narrative. This time the story a character tells really does reflect his own view of things. Bernstein's temperament and behavior anchor the film steadily in respect, dedication, and love for Kane. He enters as a traditional kind of clown, hurled noisily by a trucker he has insulted through the doorway of the *Inquirer* office; but soon we notice and like and respect his smiling protective watchfulness when Kane is standing up to Thatcher, and we have already been struck by the generosity with which he talks to Thompson about Susan and even about Leland, whom he has no reason to respect. He manifests loyalty, something in short supply around Kane, and in Everett Sloane's accurately scaled performance, which is vivid almost to the point of caricature but never crosses the line, Bernstein's warmth becomes a major player in the film's repertory of attitudes, and a surprisingly interesting one. His perspective governs his narrative in another respect, since the exuberance and charm of the early days at the newspaper come to us largely through Bernstein's eyes.

The best-known instances of multiple perspective in *Citizen Kane* involve Susan. Her operatic debut and her decision to leave Kane both come in two versions, first in Leland's, then in hers. We see her singing career first from an external point of view, telescoped in a kind of newsreel. Two big headlines, "Kane Marries Singer" and "Kane Builds Opera House," lead to a tight close-up of Susan on the stage of the new opera house, with the curtain closed for an intermission; she is heavily made up, almost hysterical for several reasons, not least the apparent fury with which she is being hectored by a man we learn later is her singing teacher, Signor Matiste (Fortunio Bonanova). A multitude of attendants are preparing her makeup and costume for the next scene; other functionaries are rushing about doing backstage tasks; and then, as the music gathers to a climax, a light that had been lowered directly above her to illuminate these preparations is swiftly raised, the attendants disappear, the curtain rises, and the camera grants us a view of Susan starting to sing – but for only a moment, because it follows instead the upward movement of the curtain to make a big, cheerful joke about the whole ridiculous business. As we slowly pan up above the commotion on stage, we pass ropes and sets for other operas stored away, waiting to be lowered into place, all the paraphernalia of backstage opera, until we finally discover on a catwalk, far above Susan, critics of great authority – two stagehands, one of whom slowly puts his fingers up to hold his nose.

When we see Susan's debut from her own perspective, after we have gained a more complicated sense of her through Thompson's questioning, things are much more painful. We see what has led up to the debut in agonizing detail. We see Matiste's attempt to give Susan's thin, weak, uncertain voice some body and color, and very soon, though not too soon, we see him announce the hopelessness of his task. It is a painful scene because of Susan's inadequacy, but it is brashly enlivened by Matiste's demonstration, in his own richly schooled voice, of what a scale ought to sound like, followed by his superb summation, "Some people can sing. Some can't. Impossible. Impossible." And when we watch him being smoothly bullied by Kane into continuing the project, the effect of course is just the opposite of giving us confidence in it. In the earlier version, we had approached the first shot of Susan at her debut with apprehension, but now we simply know what's going to happen. The second version begins with the same shots as before – Susan's hysterical, over-made-up face and Matiste's scolding (now we know who he is). This time, though, the camera begins to watch the scene from the back, which is in a way from Susan's perspective, instead of the front. The same things happen – the light disappears, the attendants vanish – but now when the curtain rises in the midst of all this anxiety, we are watching the terrible event from Susan's point of view, and having the same experience she is having.

What she sees is a palpable objectification of her anxiety. Instead of catching even one glimpse of the individual people that make up an audience, she sees only a great black undifferentiated void, a vertiginous hole in space, lit only by spotlights on the rims of the balconies. And we believe this is exactly what she would see. It is a locus classicus of Welles's imagination, and its originality remains undimmed. Nobody ever saw anything like it before, and it has become too famous to imitate. We knew about Susan's anxiety before, even felt for her, but through the powerful concreteness of this image of nothingness we pass beyond knowing into realizing. Thus it is through the strange instrument of that black void that we make contact with Susan's tortured inner life, that we feel the anxiety and fear she is feeling. The image makes its effect quickly, but not before this piece of artifice, this special effect, this gimmick, has awakened our imagination and our sympathy. From now on we are with Susan, even at the most embarrassing moments when, bent over like an old crone, she tries with infinite ineptitude to arrange the giant flower displays Kane has had sent – at those moments, our pity becomes excruciating, and we begin to feel almost ashamed to be watching her suffer. But we nevertheless stay with her in feeling because the film has made us know exactly what she's feeling.

When Susan's debut comes to us from her point of view, what we see isn't limited to what she herself sees, nor is it obliged to be in the convention the film is using. She doesn't see the entire staff of *The Inquirer* trying to stay awake in their tuxedos. She doesn't see Kane's fury at the whispered laughter and derogation in the audience, his face set in stone, his stubborn applause. It is only we who see him try to deny and destroy the failure by the violence and stubbornness of his belief and of his will. And yet these images are connected with Susan's point of view in the sense that they are in balance with her fear and anxiety – she doesn't see them, and she doesn't exactly imagine them, but they are concrete parts of the world before which she knows she is making a fool of herself.

It is also only we who can peer down from the balcony or boxes into the orchestra seats to see another reaction to Kane's failure: Leland shredding his program in boredom. Leland's contempt generates the thrillingly intense scene that follows, which begins with Kane's staff, gathered in the office of *The Inquirer,* conferring to make sure that the paper is covering Susan's debut as Mr. Kane would wish it. Kane himself enters in a sumptuous opera coat, an extraordinary figure of power, but deeply depressed – he is making himself go through the motions of will, but his energy is gone. All the notices are ready, he is told, and they all say the right things, except the review from the drama critic – Leland's, which he is supposedly still writing behind a closed door at the end of the long room. The whole scene is dense with deep focus and chiaroscuro. When Kane finds Leland drunkenly asleep over his typewriter, he asks Bernstein to read the two sentences Leland had managed to write before he passed out. They are couched in the tone of high scorn traditional for journalists devastating a flop, and their contempt pains Bernstein; but not Kane, whom in fact they galvanize into finishing the review in the syle in which Leland began it, plunging violently into this extraordinary act of theater, of wit, of revenge, justice, and self-destruction. When Leland comes to and tells Bernstein, in an almost childish voice, "I knew I'd never get that through," he is rebuked by Bernstein's proudly telling him that Kane is finishing the review exactly as Leland would have written it. When Leland, still far from sober, then approaches Kane, saying, "Hello, Charlie. I didn't know we were speaking," Kane answers, "Sure we're speaking, Jedediah. You're fired."

When Kane locked himself into the project of making Susan into an opera star, the clear impossibility of the project turned him into an automaton of fixed will, as is visible in the way he applauds at the premiere – there is no other way to keep on going. But the inspired idea of mimicking Leland's contempt for his project excites him into life, and he again becomes interesting to watch: focused, purposeful, commanding a curiosity that's close to sympathy. And the scene with Susan that follows justifies our curiosity and gets something close to sympathy, for it forms one of the film's most original and subtle dialectical turnings, in texture and tone, and it delicately shifts the film's balance of sympathies.

While Susan is sitting on the floor, reading the newspaper notices of her performance spread out before her, she comes across *The Inquirer*'s annihilating attack. While she is screaming her fury at what she takes to be Leland's review – "Stop telling me he's your friend. A friend don't write that kind of review" – Kane winces but tries not to pay attention: "That'll be enough, Susan," the routine parental rebuke suggesting that he has dealt with such behavior often before. He answers a knock on the door and gets a hand-delivered letter from Leland, whom he had fired the night before, but to whom he had afterward sent a check for $25,000; the letter contains the check, torn to little pieces, together with Leland's prized copy of the idealistic "Declaration of Principles" that Kane had written for the first edition of *The Inquirer* – a document Kane now wryly calls "an antique." Still screaming at a punishing pitch of shrillness, Susan asks whether what she had heard about the check is true, and Kane answers that it is. But during this exchange, what catches the camera's attention and ours is the impassivity with which he slowly shakes the pieces of the check out of the envelope. Now Susan, who has had no adequate response to what she suffered at the premiere and what she is suffering now as she reads the contemptuous reviews, announces provocatively that she has decided not to sing any more. Kane refuses, of course, and the terms of his refusal don't acknowledge even that she has a role in the matter: "I don't propose to have myself made ridiculous." When she answers, "What about me? I'm the one that's got to do the singing. I'm the one that gets the razzberries," he answers her complaints, which we find appealing to the point of being heartbreaking, with surreal bureaucratic formality, as if he were a corporation comprising many separate entities that report their activities formally to each other: "My reasons satisfy me, Susan. You seem unable to understand them. I will not tell them to you again." And he comes to stand beside her, casting his shadow over her, so that for a moment one sees only the whites of her eyes. Then she gives in.

We come to this appalling scene fresh from having given almost unqualified sympathy to Susan at the premiere. We had winced at her low breeziness with the reporters right after the marriage, telling them "Charlie" is going to do this and "Charlie" is going to do that. Now we are staggered by her vulgarity, her shrill rage, her huge capacity to make herself unbearable. But the inspired and courageous ugliness of the scene makes it the vehicle through which we arrive at a new attitude toward Kane. How can he stand her? The fact that we can ask the question shows that some shifting of sympathy is taking place – we are moving into a new way of seeing Kane. Not for what he actually does, especially to Susan – this remains repellent. His refusal to give up the project of her career despite her suffering is more of the thick egotism that we have seen enough of. Yet as the scene does its work on us, something in Kane's behavior begins to qualify and reshape our antipathy toward him, bringing us into a new attitude that, although it plays its role in the film's dialectic, isn't quite contrast, or contradiction. We read in Kane's impassivity in the face of failure and of Susan's shrill complaints, not the woodenness of the automaton, but the possibility of a nobler stoicism and even signs of suffering. We make a kind of contact with him, though not the kind that would move in understanding along with his inner desires and fears, and see the world from his point of view. The contact we feel here is like realizing the concreteness of an object in the physical world. Suddenly, we sense a three-dimensionality in Kane's impassivity, a sense of the pressure inside him, which our sympathetic imagination can't help responding to by acknowledging. The effect is due partly to his (and Welles's) physical size, which throughout the film has had a subliminal expressive effect on us beyond rational justification. And now the film's bizarre and deep inspiration is to extend this invitation to sympathy just as Kane is most cruelly forcing his will on Susan to continue her career.

In the next move of this new and oddly delicate dialectic of our feelings about Kane, his behavior after Susan's suicide attempt astonishes us by being softly tender. We aren't tempted to generalize – that he has learned compassion through suffering. Yet when Kane's face comes close to Susan and to us, its touchingly round and unguarded softness seems to signal a great event, registering a great change. He keeps watch over her drugged sleep in a slumped posture eloquently expressive of defeat, but also of faithfulness and concern. When she does wake up we hardly know what to expect, but what we don't expect is that she should turn to him in such dircct and confiding explanation: "Charlie, I couldn't make you see how I felt. . . . You don't know what it means to feel that the whole audience doesn't want you." That confession – "to feel that the whole audience doesn't want you" – is heartbreaking in its honesty and courage, and, incidentally, a thrilling piece of writing. (At moments like this we see that it's far more than an academic matter to want to find out who wrote what in this disputed script – one wants to know exactly whom to admire.) He replies, with equal directness, "That's when you've got to fight them!" The slogan sounds as if it comes from his own personal, rather boyish code, and he surely means it, but he doesn't insist on it for even a moment, and his face softens even more as he gives up the code and the fight, gives in to Susan, and for her. His pity is a marvelously invented and realized movement in the film's dialectic. And it simply doesn't connect with his willful forcing of Susan in the previous scene – that happened, now this happens, yet nothing feels incoherent or unrealized. This is the normal logic of the film, but it never has greater authority than here, nor is more moving. But the crushing truth is that the dialectic still has in store for us a terrible antithesis, the last episode in the Susan–Kane story, in which he tears her room, her bed, and by proxy her body and very being, into pieces after she defies his will by leaving him.

Yet, in another of the film's most inspired moves, we find that pathos is far from the last word about Susan. There was so much wit and invention on hand during the making of *Citizen Kane* that it could afford as an unexpected dividend the verbal wising-up generously granted to Susan. Toward the end she gets some of the sharpest lines in the film, and she knows how good they are. When the disastrous opera tour is finished, Kane turns his attention, and his will, to his new project of creating the monstrous Xanadu, and when the couple are installed there, Susan's discontent expresses itself not only in her addiction to jigsaw puzzles but in some savvy wisecracks. During a domestic interlude, with Susan at her puzzle and Kane cozily warming himself by standing right inside the gigantic fireplace ("Our home is here, Susan") – he thinks dreamily back to his newspaper days: "The bulldog's just gone to press," to which Susan ripostes, "Well, hurray for the bulldog!" He pays no attention, of course. When he proposes a pointless picnic to the Everglades, her objection is practical, and her bad English a form of wit: "Who wants to sleep in tents when they've got a nice room of their own, with their own bath, where they know where everything is?" They have the picnic anyway, and a big fight in their tent, where Kane himself gets off a first-rate wisecrack that satirizes the huge echo chambers in his own precious Xanadu: "You're in a tent, darling, we're not at home. I can hear you very well if you speak in a normal tone of voice." But when he soon afterward slaps her following her devastating critique of his inability to love and of his whole way of life – a hideous moment – she scores the final point with

Susan (Comingore) at Xanadu, with one of her jigsaw puzzles. (Photo courtesy of Photofest)

a stroke of deep wisdom about how people work: "Don't tell me you're sorry." His weak "I'm not sorry" signals not rebuttal but checkmate. After Kane's death her taste for wisecracks remains, when she says good-bye to Thompson: "Come around and tell me the story of your life some time" – she is making a joke and making a pass, smilingly aware of both possibilities. Who could have predicted how *nice* she would turn out to be?

The double version of Susan's leaving Kane is less clear-cut in meaning and effect than the double version of her singing career. The fight with Kane in the tent at the picnic, and its climax in Kane's slap, seems to be what crystallized Susan's decision to leave; she made the decision thoughtfully, planning to say a calm good-bye to Kane but only to him, which she collectedly proceeds to do. Kane's reaction brings forth a truly virtuoso performance by Welles, rich with rhetorical shadings. At first he weakly attempts to command, "I won't let you go"; he then modulates to poignant, almost tearful pleading, "Please don't go. Please, Susan," then sinks to a self-abnegating murmur, "You mustn't go." But these convincing and

"I can't do this to you? Oh, yes, I can." (Photo courtesy of Photofest)

moving attempts at persuasion are only the prelude to what we know will follow: his inevitable yielding to his own accustomed point of view, "You can't do this to me." Susan welcomes this with a cry of smiling vindictive joy, which she seems to have had ready all along to answer what she too knew would happen: "I see, it's you that this is being done to. It's not me at all. Not what it means to me. I can't do this to you? Oh, yes, I can." And then from Kane's perspective we see her walking away through an elaborate archway, opening a door beyond and passing slowly through it into the shadows. The shot is held for a long moment, but there is no sense of finality; this isn't the end of the story of Kane and Susan. In fact, as we have come to expect in this dialectically organized film, the shot of Susan's departure from Kane's perspective is soon balanced by a reverse shot, looking back toward Kane standing in the doorway, watching her leave.

The reverse shot is actually part of the perspective not of Susan but of the unsavory Raymond, Kane's butler, whose contempt for his employer is virtually our final take on Kane, and therefore something of a gamble on the part of a film that has presented so complexly qualified a portrait: "Well, like I tell you, the old man acted kind of funny sometimes, but I knew how to handle him." Raymond's narrative begins when he almost runs into Susan at a right angle, when she is leaving; he looks for the cause of her action, and sees, down a much amplified series of arches, Kane at the doorway. And it is through Raymond's narrative that we learn that Kane's standing motionless in the doorway of Susan's room didn't mean acceptance but preparation for vengeance. The vengeance begins with the famous cry of the white cockatoo, a complete newcomer to the film, which has been strenuously interpreted – understandably so, since it lies so far outside the normal range of imagery and tonality of the film, that it can't help seeming unusually portentous. (Pauline Kael [76–9] argues plausibly that the cockatoo, together with Kane's bald-headed makeup, is imported from Peter Lorre's *Mad Love*.) Whatever it means, wherever it comes from, it accurately prophesies the emotional temperature of what follows: Kane's expression of fury at Susan's rebellion by tearing her room apart, destroying her luggage, her bed, her knickknacks, her books, everything in the daintily and elegantly decorated room, with its tasteful Pompeian motifs, so poignantly indicative of what she has learned. Kane visits his destruction on Susan's very body. We feel glad that nobody is watching this awful happening, apart from us – which is both true and not true, for the repellent Raymond is watching, though we're not aware of him. But when Kane, his rage winding down, finds the paperweight and emerges with it from the room, the entire staff of Xanadu including Raymond has assembled, like people watching an accident on the street.

Kane doesn't notice them, they mean nothing to him; he moves away from the violence into what seems like peace, walking through another series of arches, the enclosures for mirrors in which his figure is reflected to infinity. The way he holds himself shows that he has been calmed by the power of the paperweight and the magic word "Rosebud" that it has brought up into his consciousness; one can just make out that he is smiling. The infinite reflection of his image in the mirrors isn't satiric, not in the least critical of the egotism that built the castle with such grandiose effects. The repetition of the motif of arches has a valedictory implication, connected as it is with Kane's pace and posture and his smile. The same is true of the multiple reflections of Kane himself in the mirrors, the repetition of his own image, past which he makes his way. These reflections and repetitions, normal in the film's idiom, give us so extended a view of

"One can just make out that he is smiling." (Photo courtesy of Photofest)

Kane that they seem to connect the film's parts with each other and sum up the whole structure.

Jedediah Leland stands in the most oblique relation to the film's dialectic of any of the characters or motifs. Thompson's interview with him in the retirement home is the longest of the interviews, and its presentation of the character's point of view the most fully worked out; and this seems right, for Leland was Kane's oldest and supposedly closest friend. The interview is divided into sections, but it returns to the original setting and to Leland's verbal account of Kane after each piece of the narrative it generates; these returns make Leland and his views a major presence in the film. But the first narrative, which begins after Leland's "It was a marriage just like any other marriage," immediately casts doubt on Leland's trustworthiness as a reporter. What Leland says represents not a fact but a chosen tone, his special brand of bored irony, which is therefore a good introduction to his character and his point of view but not a valid report about Kane or his marriage. The showpiece of cinematic magic and art at the Kane breakfast table that immediately follows sets Leland's bored viewpoint aside completely in favor of a more observant and complex reading of the marriage sponsored by the film itself. In fact, however much we see and hear him, Leland's point of view is rarely validated. When Thompson asks Leland about Susan, he responds with characteristic off-hand malice, "You know what Charlie called her? The day after he'd met her, he told me about her. He said she was a cross-section of the American public." We take this as literally true, but when we ourselves see Kane meeting Susan it is clear that he is deeply touched by her, and nothing else in the film contradicts this.

Leland talks about Kane in the interview with Thompson with articulate, practiced, and above all calm hostility. But he doesn't refer to a crucial confrontation he had with Kane, which is perhaps the most complexly dramatic episode of the film. The confrontation turns out to focus not primarily on Leland but on Kane, and it resembles the scene after Susan's debut by qualifying and complicating our attitude toward Kane. The common element is Kane's holding back, his restraint, when attacked.

This is one of the few scenes of traditional dramatic complexity in the film, with richly rendered personal relations between the characters, asking us to be aware of what the characters are thinking about each other, and asking us to speculate why. Traditional dramatic complexity might seem out of place in the idiom of *Citizen Kane,* too traditional, too literary for so artificial and emphatically cinematic a style. But the confrontation scene in many respects fits right into the style of the rest of *Citizen Kane* – it is full of devices and special effects. The famous experiment of putting ceilings on the sets is unusually noticeable here, and it effectively increases the sense of dramatic pressure inside the room. Deep focus, one of the elements people remember best from *Citizen Kane* and an eloquently expressive device throughout the film, seems in this scene perfectly natural and useful, for it is completely in tune with the psychological distance between Kane and Leland. Another of Welles and Toland's habits, noted with amusement by critics and audiences alike, is here too – their love for photographing from bizarre angles. The confrontation between Kane and Leland is seen more or less from beneath the floor, a peculiar choice, admittedly, but one with the useful expressive effect of setting the characters up on a stage, thereby sharpening the intensity with which we look at them.

At the beginning of the scene, we expect a showdown, and in part we get one. Leland has been drinking steadily after the election, and when he finally enters the large room where Kane is wearily getting ready to go home, he has brought himself to the point of daring to voice the moral charges against Kane that he has been storing up – Kane's egotism, lack of concern for others, greed for power, stupid and self-involved ignorance of the economic and political realities of his world, and most important, his inability to love. He is saying what he has been unready or afraid to say before; and the film itself has never before explicitly made this indictment, though we know the general charges and are in essential agreement with them.

Kane asks not to have to hear what Leland has to say, but mildly and with courtesy: "Well, if you've got drunk to talk to me about Miss Alexander, don't bother. I'm not interested." But Leland proceeds with full malice, and the hostility in his goading, though it gives the accusation power, might take away its authority, were it not that the film never denies that Kane has behaved badly with regard to his wife and son, and to his campaign. Still, something studied in Leland's self-conscious language keeps us from giving him our full sympathy: "As long as I can remember, you've talked about giving the people their rights as if you could make them a present of liberty, as a reward for services rendered." The scenario undercuts Leland's authority by giving him a highly uncertain tone, drunk or not: "You remember the workingman? . . . He's turning into something called organized labor. . . . Charlie, when your precious underprivileged really get together – oh, boy, that's going to add up to something bigger than your privilege, and then I don't know what you'll do. Sail away to a desert island, probably, and lord it over the monkeys." He is shrewd about the rise of the unions, but the speech loses our sympathy through its sappy and foolish ending. When Kane answers, "I wouldn't worry about it too much, Jed. There'll probably be a few of them there to let me know when I do something wrong," we begin to hear a forbearance, a reluctance to quarrel, a desire to keep in touch, that is close to magnanimity. He could stop the flow of Leland's hostility at any time, you are sure, but he doesn't choose to, and wondering why this should be true certainly doesn't diminish our respect for him.

To enforce these implications, Welles's tone and his whole manner toward Leland exhibit a certain warmth and a moving willingness to allow himself to be vulnerable. At first he seems merely patient with a drunken friend, but his restraint gradually becomes more interesting than that. His one ineffectual attempt to break off Leland's attack – "Aw, go on home" – almost underlines his rejection of anger. We become increasingly eager to know what he is feeling, and the fact that we keep on not learning begins paradoxically to create in us a sense of his inner life, though one with which we can make no contact.

Kane's holding himself in makes his thoughts and feelings seem to lie deep within him, and that gives them force and weight. His silence generates our concrete sense of the "within" of his inner life, the silence becomes the "within," and in this process he gathers density with the effect of gathering value. His silence lets us believe he is experiencing the confrontation with Leland with the same attitude as our own. All these considerations finally swing the balance of our sympathy decisively in his favor, and when at the end he consents to drink with Leland – "A toast, Jedediah, to love on my terms. Those are the only terms anybody ever knows, his own" – the phrasing and placing of the plain words give them not only power but authority. Bitter in his cynicism, unacquainted with love and perhaps incapable of love – he may be all of this, but what he has just spoken is what his life and observations have taught him. His uninflated words, in this context and to this friend, and in Welles's now almost nonrhetorical delivery, come through as the voice of actual experience, the voice of true feeling, against which Leland's judgments ring thin and even false, moralistic out of mere conventionality, if not out of malice and resentment.

And we aren't really surprised at this. Throughout the film, Leland has been asked by the scenario to speak with such insistent irony as to risk overload. It's a chancy calculation: Why don't we weary of his irony? Why don't we rebel? In fact we come close to rebelling in the nursing home, where his relentlessly malicious view of Kane comes to seem not only emasculated and tired but cheap: "Five years ago he wrote me from that place down in the South, what's it called? Shangri-La? El Dorado? Sloppy Joe's?" And some of the weapons he tries to use are too sharp for him to handle: "Of course, a lot of us check out without having any special convictions about death. But we do know what we're leaving. We do believe in something." For this hollow piety the film undercuts him cruelly in his next speech: "You're absolutely sure you haven't got a cigar?"

In the Kane–Leland relation Kane has always been the vital partner. The question right at the beginning of the film as to what assignment Leland is to have on the newspaper hints at many kinds of insufficiency – of will, of concentration, of interest, of energy, of life. And we note again and again, if only out of the corner of our eye, his lack of personal relations with anybody besides Kane, his lack of a sexual identity in particular, and this vague observation colors our sense of him at almost every moment. He hovers in Kane's orbit to be near that energy and life, to feed on it, and this surely diminishes his authority as a judge, though his accusing Kane of misuse of power is accurate, and we can never fully write it off as due to envy or a sense of inferiority. It is an ambitiously conceived characterization, and if the way it plays out isn't perfectly clear, that doesn't diminish the size of Leland's role in the film, nor even the effectiveness of the character. Our understanding of him and his motives comes and goes, and so does our sympathy. We share his contempt for Kane's talk about *his* "people"; we too wince when Kane accuses Gettys and Emily of wanting "to take the love of the people of this state away from [him]." We understand why Leland wants to be allowed to work on the Chicago paper – to get away and protect himself from this windbag, this champion egotist, this blindly willful colleague and friend of so many years, who has such power over him. But it seems infinitely mean-spirited of him to make the demand at this moment, when Kane is not only discouraged but showing uncharacteristic restraint and even a pleading affection for Leland himself.

Though all of Kane's people have opinions about him, only Leland is given space and time to articulate a developed view. His analysis of Kane, discolored by dislike and envy as it is, attracts us for its sophisticated intelligence – and then repels us by its mean-spiritedness. He is the one character who tries to satisfy the need we ourselves have felt throughout the film, a need to describe Kane at length, to explain, to try to understand. He is our surrogate, and we want to be loyal to him. But all his thoughts and actions are infected by lack of passion, his lack of a strong purchase on working and living and loving. And though this confrontation scene, which almost releases Kane from criticism, doesn't cancel any of his self-serving, cruel, insensitive actions, it deprives us of a firm point of view for dealing with them. The Kane–Leland relationship in the end, however cogent Leland's criticisms may be, amplifies instead of negating the weight, the importance, the impact of Kane, who asked more of life and whose desires were infinitely stronger.

A major instance of the dialectic in *Citizen Kane,* and one very near its heart, is the manifold imagery of the aging process. Welles's visible presence in the film as actor, and his never unfelt presence as the director, make one think of all the images of aging as arising directly out of Welles's own intuitions and imaginings about what it must be like to grow old. And that puts emphasis on Welles's actual youthfulness when he made the film. The glimpses of Kane at the very beginning of the film and in *News on the March* offer images of Kane at various ages of his life. The theme of aging thus seems to emerge spontaneously, so that when the issue comes in for explicit examination, we have already had considerable dealings with it. We are all the more eager to look at the character more steadily, particularly curious to look at him as a young man – partly because Welles's youthfulness was so famous when he made the film that it's virtually part of the film. We are not disappointed. Young Kane's first appearance, at the desk in the office of *The Inquirer,* is managed with a transparent cunning worthy of young Charlie himself. Thatcher, in a fury, is holding a copy of *The Inquirer* in front of him, reading it with his habitual outrage; when he lowers it, he reveals (for the first time in the film) the very cause of that outrage, the young owner-editor-director-writer Charles Kane/Orson Welles, smiling, utterly pleased with himself, in easy control of the job and the scene – both actor and character at their most appealing. It is a glorious moment for its thrillingly engineered and richly inspired view of Welles, and also for something else it happens to introduce: the radio-trained Welles's expertise in split-second ensemble dialogue cuing, in which the characters get out of each other's way just in the nick of time, physically and vocally, often with such near-misses as to make the brilliantly clear audibility they do achieve almost impossible to credit.

All the phases of Kane's aging are richly represented, if not quite with the brio of this first appearance of young Charlie. Welles seems to have taken it as a special challenge to get the expressive most and best out of the various phases of makeup and costume he has assigned himself. Kane's aging was clearly one of the major projects of the enterprise, and just as clearly something that touched Welles's imagination deeply. But when it comes to the representation of Kane's very old age, at Xanadu, Pauline Kael's objections are unanswerable: "the make-up was erratic and waxy (especially in the bald-headed scenes, such as the one in the picnic tent) . . . there are times when the magic of movies fails. The camera comes so close that it can reveal too much. Kane as an old man was an actor trying to look old" (73). And there's another technical point to add to Kael's account – the decision to use heavy makeup to set Kane's eyes far back in his head makes them almost inexpressive, depriving Welles of one of his great resources. It's hard to see how this happened to so canny a theatrical operator.

In the last sequence in the film, when the journalists have gathered at Xanadu for a postmortem of Kane and of their own investigations, we inevitably conduct postmortems of our own thoughts about Kane, his whole experience and the whole film. We will do well to get "Rosebud" out of

The makeup for Kane's old age. (Photo courtesy of Photofest)

the way first. All the abuse the device has got through the years for superficiality and glibness is understandable enough; yet the way it delivers its meaning and that meaning itself are so transparently simple and pleased with themselves that it is hard to see why people who are taking the film in the spirit in which it is offered can make heavy weather out of their scorn for it. The problem seems to lie in the gap between the richness of the idea of loss and the tinny actuality of the sled; Kael doesn't resist the temptation to do one of her favorite numbers on it – imagining people who are deeply impressed with this "meaning," making up what they might say about it, and then crucifying them for doing so (59–60). But the flair with which the revelation is accomplished – the immense array of junk, the drama of our watching and wondering what we're watching for, the noisy crescendo of Herrmann's music, the commotion of the workmen's movements, the just-glimpsed identity of the end of the quest – all these give an assured theatrical sendoff to the idea, and fit in perfectly with the ironic mode of much of the film.

In any case, the gimmick of the ending is only part of a very impressive scene, visually. The eye fills with the scale of the last scene, its crowded emptiness, the accumulation of objects that once were meaningful but aren't any more. And this huge fact is revealed to us by the masterly slow sweep of the camera's scrutiny of all these things, moving by many, many objects we don't recognize, but also moving without pause past objects we do recognize. The camera owns this scene – the presence of the workmen doesn't alter the fact that *there is nobody here*. Nobody but us.

The references to jigsaw puzzles here and elsewhere in the film are usually lightweight self-satires of the film's famous structure, but here they accomplish something more. When Thompson says that he has been "playing with a jigsaw puzzle," he implies he has learned nothing about Kane – it is a theatrical gesture of casual skepticism and practiced professional disbelief in "the truth." But the film's dialectic has accustomed us to expect an antithesis to follow every thesis, so even as we hear Thompson and the other journalists deny that they have learned anything, we ourselves propose to believe that we have learned and understood a great deal. And the dialectic continues. We have the privilege of being left alone in the great hall, which implies that a major event is about to happen. When the identity of Rosebud and perhaps of Kane himself is revealed, it is to us alone, it is only we who are in the inner sanctum of the secret. We alone watch the oblivious workmen throw Charlie's old sled on the fire, and we alone watch its paint curl up and disappear in the flames, but not before we catch a glimpse of the yearned-for word. Here then is the antithesis to the great revelation we have expected – the triviality of the actual object identified by the word. Its meaning barely exists, yet it is a powerful and immensely successful moment. We have learned what we have learned, whatever it might be, whatever it might mean, however important it might be. But even as we realize that we are again being toyed with by smart alecks, by illusion artists, the revelatory device interlocks so marvelously with other devices in this film full of devices, that it wields an unarguable power. It isn't an answer – answers aren't Welles's thing and certainly not this film's thing – but what was wanted was an ending, and this is definitely an ending.

3

The Magnificent Ambersons

Diaghilev, commissioning the scenario for a ballet from Jean Cocteau, made one stipulation: "*Étonnez-moi.*" When Welles had to choose the subject for his first film at RKO Radio, he may have felt a little like Cocteau. But the search he and Herman J. Mankiewicz conducted did in fact yield something astonishing and exhilarating – *Citizen Kane*. To find a subject for his second film was a less focused and shapely affair: Welles sifted through many ideas, hunting for one that would feed his imagination. This had been his method when he was working in the Federal Theatre Project, the Mercury Theatre, and in radio, and it's the procedure of most artists, few of whom gestate their projects in long meditation of a single possibility. Film as a medium, as an art, and as a business, doesn't welcome or foster extended rumination. The search for a subject after *Kane* proved more uncertain than anything Welles had undergone before.

First, for Dolores del Rio, with whom he was having an affair at the time, Welles wrote a screenplay about Nazis in Mexico, tentatively titled *Mexican Melodrama,* but the Mexican government refused permission to film it in Mexico, and Welles gave it up. He briefly considered a Ben Hecht script for *Cyrano de Bergerac,* and then was diverted to the more piquant idea of directing Chaplin in a film about the celebrated Landru, the modern French Bluebeard who murdered a whole series of wives. Chaplin rejected this, perhaps because he didn't want to act under Welles's direction, but he bought Welles's material and story line and later fashioned them himself into *Monsieur Verdoux*. Welles adapted Eric Ambler's *Journey into Fear* for film, as he had planned and scheduled, but he did it with his left hand, having already decided not to direct the film himself. He then came up with an unusual project that was to preoccupy him for many years: a half-fiction, half-documentary film, to be called *It's All True,* with a section about jazz, involving the life of Louis Armstrong, coauthored with Duke Ellington. RKO understandably didn't regard this unclassifiable subject as the right one for their expensive genius's second film. Finally Welles revisited material he had dramatized for radio in 1939, Booth Tarkington's novel *The Magnificent Ambersons.*

It looks like a choice of last resort, and Welles's unusual faithfulness to the novel, to the point of using much of Tarkington's actual language, might suggest that he was marking time with a run-of-the-mill project. But *The Magnificent Ambersons* called forth unexpected gifts and skills in him, or created them, as the film's intensity proves, and the material obviously touched his memory and imagination deeply. The project seems also to have appealed to his interest and ambition as a craftsman, concerned with depth of workmanship, finish of texture, and completeness of realization. Welles's film shows his love not only for Tarkington's novel but for its tone, which he made a major element of the film by taking on the role of narrator himself, rather than acting in the film. *The Magnificent Ambersons* is a great film, one of the keystones of Welles's oeuvre, a film by which one measures his worth as an artist and as a man, a worthy successor to *Citizen Kane.* If the mild, sad Tarkington novel seems a dangerous choice after the brilliant, risk-taking *Citizen Kane,* Welles was resilient and inventive; he understood his new material well, he had the confidence of youth and genius that he would find a way to deal with it, and he succeeded brilliantly.

Booth Tarkington's novel had won the Pulitzer Prize when first published in 1918 and had gone through many editions, though its reputation doesn't seem to have remained strong in 1940. Tarkington's work in general was widely known; he had become a leader of middlebrow American culture through his *Saturday Evening Post* stories about a tame, almost cute descendent of Huckleberry Finn named Penrod – both the boy and his life seemed made to order for Norman Rockwell's illustrations. The Penrod stories were pleasingly nostalgic for innocent boyhood in peaceful small-town America, but the nostalgia *of The Magnificent Ambersons* was more ambiguous and more melancholy.

The Magnificent Ambersons deals with the decline in vitality, power, and prestige of the grand family of a Midwestern town around the turn of the twentieth century. They are the chief landowners in their town, but they lose everything, because they can't handle or even notice the fact that the town is growing and spreading, devaluing their own property holdings, as new money moves into new streets and new houses. The new streets are needed partly because of the automobile, which figures largely in the story since one of the leading characters, Eugene Morgan (Joseph Cotten), is involved in its production.

The confusion in the familial and romantic relations of the characters is connected with their economic decline, but it isn't an obvious connection and is never emphasized, and this lack of explicitness is actually a strength in both novel and film – one feels the interrelationship vaguely but deeply. At the opening, Isabel (Dolores Costello), the only daughter of the Ambersons, is engaged to the poor but gifted Eugene; but while serenading her tipsily one evening, he falls backward into his bass fiddle – foolish misbehavior that displeases Isabel to a puzzlingly excessive degree. (The excessiveness of her feelings is to show up later in her relation to her son.) She breaks off the engagement and marries a milquetoast named Wilbur Minafer (Don Dillaway), by whom she has one child – the scion of the Ambersons, George (Tim Holt), whom, as the town prophetess predicts, Isabel spoils badly. By the age of about twenty, George has become insufferably arrogant and opinionated.

The main action of the film begins when the Ambersons give one of their famous balls in George's honor when he is home for vacation from his Eastern college. Among the many friends and acquaintances who have been invited (far more of them than the arrogant George approves of), is Eugene Morgan, who has returned to town as a highly successful part-inventor and developer of a horseless carriage and the widowed father of a daughter, Lucy (Anne Baxter), who is the same age as George. The family patriarch, Major Amberson (Richard Bennett), is the chief host, joined by the other members of the household, which includes, besides Isabel and Wilbur, the Major's unmarried son, Jack (Ray Collins), and Wilbur's unmarried sister, Fanny (Agnes Moorehead). Eugene's reappearance is a happy event for everybody except George, whose instinctive animosity to him generates the action of the film. Every sign of familiarity and affection between Eugene and his mother disgusts George, though he is strongly attracted to Eugene's daughter, Lucy.

When Wilbur dies prematurely and Eugene renews his courtship of Isabel, George sets out to destroy a relationship that he finds almost unspeakably wrong. It seems horrible to him that the marriage of his mother and Eugene might show that they had been in love all along, even while she was married to his father. But that explanation doesn't quite account for the degree to which the very idea of his mother's remarriage is repugnant to him. Tarkington tentatively draws a parallel between the triangular drama involving George, his mother, and Eugene, and Shakespeare's triangular drama involving Hamlet, his mother, and Claudius, and it is also hard to avoid considering Freud's Oedipus complex. But Welles didn't take up these hints; he treated the emotional drama of conflict entirely in terms of character in a traditional way. The character mainly in question is Isabel's. George's destructive efforts wouldn't work were it not for her beautiful but strange yieldingness, her constant soft anxiety about George's health and general welfare, her ineffectuality, her inability to ask anything for herself – qualities that help us understand the love everybody feels for her, and also help us understand how impossible it would be for Eugene to try to force her into any action favorable to his suit. These qualities in the end doom her to the weak and self-defeating submissiveness to George's will that destroys her chance for happiness and finally kills her.

Welles's strategies in developing this story differ from those he used in *Citizen Kane*. There are no playful magical devices, no dialectic of light and dark or of contrasting perspectives, no search for an answer to a puzzle that will explain everything about the main character. *The Magnificent Ambersons* progresses as conventional narrative, mounting straightforwardly to climax and then to resolution. But we do again feel the presence of Welles the performer. In fact, *The Magnificent Ambersons* offers one of the major experiences of this aspect of Welles's art, for he probably assigned himself the role of narrator because it allowed him at the very opening of the film to create an entire theater all by himself, through the manipulations of his own voice.

Welles's voice was never more central to his identity and his art as a performer than in this prologue. When, right after the unadorned block letters of the title, we hear that unmistakable timbre in the dark theater, while the screen is still dark, it's as if a presence has made itself a stage to appear on – Welles's voice is not only the sole presence in the theater, but the theater itself. His description of the town where the Ambersons live is Tarkington's, and the tone is Tarkington's too: amused, charmed, affectionate, patronizing, ironic without malice. But Welles's voice intensifies Tarkington's meanings and effects, and the persuasive power of his always seductive voice has in this case been heightened by the expertise of the sound technicians, who were beyond a doubt following the exact instructions they got from the young man who had at an early age proved himself in radio to be the master of sound.

We hear his voice at other junctures in the film, notably at the very end of the credits, in a passage that has become famous, though not always in admiration. People who have hardly any experience of Welles's work like to quote his final words from *The Magnificent Ambersons* and try to imitate their intonation: "I wrote the script and directed it. My name is

At the great Amberson ball, Uncle John (Charles Phipps), at right, gets embarrassingly drunk. His niece and nephew, Wilbur Minafer (Don Dillaway) and his sister Fanny (Agnes Moorehead), are dealing with him here – while George (Tim Holt) and Lucy (Anne Baxter) look on at left. The scene was cut from the final film, but the splendor this still suggests survived. (Photo courtesy of Photofest)

Orson Welles. This is a Mercury Production." Self-advertisement on this scale is close to the parody it has led to, but it feels mischievous rather than pompous, and is probably both – Welles gets away with it in this intense and serious drama because of the frank theatrical mode of the whole enterprise.

The opening description of the Ambersons' town and era is illustrated onscreen by vignettes of the life in the town. There is a fashion parade of the changes in men's clothing during the period, modeled with amusement by Joseph Cotten – or is it Eugene Morgan, the character Cotten plays in the story? (The film shifts playfully in and out of illusion.) Some colloquies among townspeople about the grandeur of the Ambersons, about Isabel's rejection of Morgan and choice of Wilbur Minafer, and about George, the spoiled heir, look like gigantic still photographs in texture, with luminous pearl-gray backgrounds against which the large, almost motionless faces of the townspeople present the superlegibility of their characters. The monumentality of the anonymous faces is right – it is in view of these critics that the magnificent Ambersons must conduct their lives. The vignettes of townspeople slyly include figures who aren't anonymous, though we don't recognize them yet; they are the leading figures in the action to come, and Eugene in fact is already initiating that action, which gradually gets under way during this prologue by way of his disastrous behavior during the serenade. We see Fanny Minafer, gossiping with friends in the period before she joined the family through her brother's marriage; Mrs. Johnson, who is to tell George angrily to leave her house; Mr. Bronson, who will be hit in the stomach by young Georgie and who much later and in a different spirit will hire him briefly as an apprentice lawyer. As for more important figures: the patriarchal Major's hat is knocked off by a snowball; Jack Amberson, from a barber chair, defends Isabel's choice of Wilbur; and even Isabel herself puts in an appearance, in a romantic rowboat with a suitor.

A final vignette, richly dressed and brilliantly performed, is a complete little dramatic scene in the fitting room of a dressmaker's shop, with several women attending the chief customer, who is also the chief talker, a Mrs. Foster, much appreciated for her knowledge of human nature, and by no means unaware of her authority – the narrator calls her a prophetess. The camera placement puts us right in the middle of the action with a slight twist of perspective – we have an unimpeded view of the commanding Mrs. Foster in her corset, but we see only fragments of the other women. The action celebrates the ritual of gossip – when Mrs. Foster is given her ceremonial cup of tea, it is handed up to her unexpectedly from the bottom left of the screen by an invisible votive attendant; when she moves forward to take it, Mrs. Johnson approaches from the lower right of the screen and reverentially cloaks her in the robe that seems to be de rigueur for a lady to wear while drinking tea in her corset. It is Mrs. Foster who predicts that the children of the loveless Minafer marriage will inevitably be spoiled; the narrator corrects her by pointing out that there is only one child.

Warmer than this slightly acid scene is an affectionate and nostalgic memory, earlier in the prologue, about a streetcar. The words, again from Tarkington, illustrate the neighborliness of the Ambersons' little town with a conceit about the obligingness of a streetcar:

> the car was genially accommodating: a lady could whistle to it from an upstairs window, and the car would halt at once and wait for her while she shut the window, put on her hat and cloak, went downstairs, found an umbrella, told the "girl" what to have for dinner, and came forth from the house.

Tarkington is out to charm us and is more than witty and skillful enough to succeed; the masterly rhythm of the long sentence is more than skillful – this is highly accomplished writing. Welles uses the passage word for word in the film, and delivers it with a friendly irony appropriate to Tarkington's words. And yet the effect is different. *The Magnificent Ambersons* was filmed in the studio (except for the automobile ride in the snow, which was filmed in a nearby icehouse), and we are more or less always aware of this; but the house that illustrates the above passage is more obviously than usual part of a movie set, a representation of a house – again we realize we are in a performing art, sensing that we are meant to realize that a certain illusion is being created by skillful people. The house is full size, yet it has the charm of a toy, and the glow of the backlighting suggests that we are looking at an old photograph album. While faithful to the wit of the conceit, Welles has added a self-reflexive edge that shows us the kind of art we are watching.

After the prologue, the presence of Welles the performing artist is more subtly felt. *The Magnificent Ambersons* is a powerful dramatic action, in which a strong illusion of reality is sustained. Yet as we become more and more conscious of the slow deliberate pace, of the quality of the lighting, dark more often than not, of the dramatic texture of most of the scenes, with their slow, tense, wrenching interaction of two or three characters – as these impressions gather, we recognize that we are encountering a distinct style of film art – deliberately emphatic, theatrical, highly inflected and behind the style we can't help sensing and naming its creator. The style of *The Magnificent Ambersons* has a pronounced manner and plenty of it, but to call it "mannered" is to miss its energy and freedom – there is no stale odor of the studied or the contrived.

The story begins as the wind sweeps us with Eugene and Lucy into the large, sumptuously decorated space of the Amberson mansion, full of light and people. We are entering one of the great set pieces of Welles's or indeed of any director's work – a flow of movement and character that seems to pass by chance into the range of the camera, though we also recognize the complex orchestration and choreography of highly stylized art. We see brief meetings of old friends, who identify themselves and their relationships and in doing so advance the action and our understanding of it. We follow two forward-moving narrative actions: George begins his courtship of Lucy in a long walk through the rooms and on all the levels of the great staircase, passing through many phases of mutual attraction and antagonism, the charm of the stroll broken occasionally by his anger at his mother's familiarity with Eugene; meanwhile Eugene is recommenc-

The Amberson ball is over, but Eugene (Joseph Cotten) and Isabel (Dolores Costello) are still waltzing – as George, her son, and Eugene's daughter, Lucy, watch from the staircase. (Photo courtesy of Photofest)

ing his courtship of Isabel, talking and dancing in a long duet of renewal. Right at the center of the sequence, Eugene's joy at being with Isabel again lifts the two of them to a crest of excitement and ardor that expresses itself in exhilarating fast dancing, which seems the cause of the surge of music as well as its effect. After this special moment the dance enlarges into a general movement, with many couples crossing and recrossing the large floor in a showpiece of cinematic virtuosity. And then George and Lucy dance, in counterpoint, a kind of happy and generous riposte to their parents' opening dance, entirely without rivalry. The reunion of Eugene and Isabel culminates in an unequivocally romantic finale, in which they are the last dancers on the dance floor, completely absorbed in each other.

The ball defines and embodies the easy grace, the frank unaffected courtesy, the unboastful leisure, the charm in which both the magnificence and the fate of the Ambersons are figured. The Amberson grace is reflected in the fluid editing and augmented by it. Welles claimed that he shot the whole sequence as "*one* reel without a single cut," and that the present break of the flow by one of the cuts robbed the sequence of a large

Jack (Ray Collins), right, the Ambersons' own congressman, and his old friend Eugene (Cotten) – just before the latter starts to waltz with Isabel. (Photo courtesy of Photofest)

measure of its fluency, but nobody has found good evidence for that in the fairly elaborate surviving records of how the film was made; and though one doesn't doubt that Welles achieved a more magical fluidity, what we have is good enough.

The most kinetically exciting parts of the ball scene are the beginning and, in particular, the ending. Lucy approaches her father with the unspoken suggestion that it is time to leave, and then everybody moves, in an exhilarating choreography of different speeds and different directions, toward the door, to go along with Eugene and Lucy outside to their automobile. The energy and grace of movement out of the mansion here, especially Isabel's and Fanny's as they fly to the door in excitement about so many things at once, gives this leave-taking ending the formal effect of rhyming with the wave of action that brought Eugene and Lucy on the wind into the Amberson mansion at the beginning of the ball.

The whole ball sequence has been extensively cut, in a development we shall look at later. The original included an extended discussion about George between Jack and Eugene, with Jack frankly critical and Eugene defending George out of loyalty to Isabel, and the question is how much this cut has hurt the film. But the apparatchiks who cut forty-three minutes of *The Magnificent Ambersons* were competent professionals – even the top brass, who had never done a tap of practical filmmaking, probably gained a little know-how merely through having been near films being made. Although one can easily imagine the added depth and ambiguity about George this colloquy between Jack and Eugene would have produced – some think Tim Holt's performance as the spoiled scion could use more depth – nevertheless, a different and not inestimable effect is achieved by the cut, giving up the underlining of the George question the scene would have added in favor of letting us watch more impartially. The cut dialogue would have called attention strongly to the injustice, even perversity, of George's instant animosity toward Eugene, who is so generous to him, but that meaning is attained anyway, without extra emphasis.

Another cut shows an additional, probably inadvertent but not contemptible effect achieved by those who cut the film. At my first viewing of the film I was particularly delighted by a moment during the ball when three little Dickensian townspeople hurry toward a great buffet, one woman exulting, "Here they are, here they are, Henry." I loved the way the film uninvidiously relished their excitement at getting to sample some expensive Amberson delicacy, and I think I remember crediting Welles's art with the trick of not telling us what the delicacy was. Reading the uncut script, I discover that what excited these people was nothing more exotic than olives, a delicacy extensively discussed in another cut passage. An instance like this can put one on both sides of the question of the *Amberson* cutting. It's not that one exactly believes that the bosses who cut out the dialogue about the olives had a clear idea of the effect of not telling the audience what all the excitement was about; their conception of what they were doing most likely went no further than guessing that the cut 'wouldn't matter much,' and they weren't really wrong.

After the departure of the guests, the richly festive mood of the ball peels away to reveal the tense relations among the Ambersons. Here the extraordinary acting of the film comes to the foreground of our attention. Welles was an expert on acting by this time. He is said to have shaped his Mercury players into an unprecedentedly integrated ensemble (and his actors must have taught him a lot in return). He brought several Mercury players with him to Hollywood, but apart from Joseph Cotten, Agnes Moorehead, and Ray Collins, he chose not to use any of them in *The Magnificent Ambersons*. The Mercury experience is visible in any case, through the continuous pressure of emotion and intelligence, and the pre-

In the Amberson kitchen: George teasing his Aunt Fanny while consuming her pie – with his Uncle Jack, center, about to intervene. (Photo courtesy of Photofest)

cision of the choreography, which bear witness to an exacting rehearsal procedure.

There is a marvelously played scene in the Amberson kitchen, in which George, just home from his graduation ceremony at his Eastern college, stuffs himself with Fanny's strawberry shortcake ("first of the season"). It is brilliantly written and it serves a clear narrative function, but it is the precision of the interaction between Fanny and George that gives the scene weight and intensity beyond its ostensible point about lack of communication. It's a triumph of style and stylization without leaving the realistic mode. Agnes Moorehead and Tim Holt easily establish the close though antagonistic familial rapport between aunt and nephew, which is the ground of the scene. In this case they are working at cross purposes, and trying not to show it. Everyday phrases – "Quit bolting your food!" or "Is it sweet enough?" – interrupt but do not relax the formal antiphony in which Fanny's attempt to learn more about the relation between Isabel and Eugene keeps being thwarted by George's half-stupid, half-cruel assumption that she already knows what she is trying to find out, just because he knows it himself:

> FANNY: So, uh . . . Eugene came to the station to meet you?
> GEORGE: To meet us? How could he?
> FANNY: I don't know what you mean. Want some more milk?
> GEORGE: No, thanks.
> FANNY: I haven't seen him while your mother's been away.
> GEORGE: Naturally. He's been East himself.
> FANNY: Did you see him?
> GEORGE: Naturally. Since he made the trip home with us.

"Naturally" is partly obtuse, partly intentional persecution, against which Fanny hides in expressionlessness, until Jack enters and his and George's teasing about her interest in Eugene becomes cruel and drives her to tears – a modulation magnificently engineered by the superb Moorehead.

When I first saw *The Magnificent Ambersons,* I couldn't get enough of the timing of pauses and glances in this scene. It was my first experience of completely achieved ensemble acting. I had seen ensemble acting before, but the brilliant precision of inflection in Welles's version helped me for the first time to name what I was encountering.

The task of the other actors is to convey in a more matter-of-fact way a sense of long familiarity with the Amberson culture and long association with each other. Ray Collins is so deeply and comfortably inside his role that his very figure seems to represent the culture of the Ambersons. He does virtually nothing in the film – George tells Lucy that he is in Congress because "the family always liked to have someone in Congress" – and when he appears he is almost never accomplishing a purpose, either of work or of human relations. His sizable, friendly, comfortable presence is a major asset to our sense of the value of the Amberson culture, and to the film's density of representation.

When Welles persuaded old Richard Bennett, who had acted little since he had been a major matinee idol in the theater of the 1910s and 1920s, to take the relatively small role of the family patriarch, the Major, he was following an intuition of genius, and Bennett's lack of need or desire to seek attention for himself as an actor comes to stand movingly for the virtue of the old ways. But even Welles couldn't have foreseen the sincerity and intensity Bennett brings to the death speech Tarkington invented for the old man: his meditations about the origin of man and life in the sun. Welles as narrator introduces the passage in his tenderest intonation:

"And now Major Amberson was engaged in the profoundest thinking of his life," and what Tarkington has invented for this moment in the Major's life is an entirely unexpected addition to our sense of the depth of the character:

> It must be, in the sun. . . . There wasn't anything here, but the sun in the first place . . . the sun. The earth came out of the sun . . . and we came out of the earth . . . so – but whatever we are we must have been in the earth.[1]

Joseph Cotten and Anne Baxter play outsiders, bringing wider, more sophisticated experience to thinking about and relating to the Ambersons. Joseph Cotten looks as if he has been fully ripened and smoothed over by the world, but he combines this convincingly with Eugene's renewed energy and joy at the prospect of loving Isabel again. Anne Baxter's Lucy is worldly and mature, yet convincingly young; we enjoy tracing the undercurrent of thinking and judging beneath her charming exterior – we like collaborating with her skeptical intelligence. For some viewers, her hardest task may be making credible the attraction she feels to George, despite her inevitable irritation about his bad manners, his arrogance, his self-willed stubbornness. Tim Holt's participation in achieving this effect is more likely to have been instinctive rather than deliberate, but that feels right, since his value to the film, the way he makes it work, lies not in intelligent motives but in his solid sexual force. And there is also the power with which he can exasperatingly present himself as boor and sulk.

The precious and vulnerable heart of the Amberson culture is, of course, Isabel. The magic of Dolores Costello's evanescent performance is so delicate that it almost escapes notice as the wonderfully controlled and sustained acting it in fact is. Her soft and yielding sweetness, her unasserted, unexploited beauty, the light, breathy tones of her anxiety and her nagging, her innocent eyes, so often surprised by life – eyes of which we are privileged to catch heartbreaking glimpses in a recklessly, crazily beautiful scene in which she reads Eugene's letter in the dark – Costello embodies all this with an effortless breeding worthy of the Amberson's own estimate of themselves.

The acting of the Welles players differed from ordinary Hollywood acting as widely as the general style and look of Welles's films differed from ordinary Hollywood practice. He must have known how much his style diverged from the Hollywood norm, but it's not clear how much it mattered to him. The sources of his style as actor, director, and cinematographer – his "art film" style, some might call it – have been located in the

German expressionistic movies of the twenties, those of Lang, Murnau, and others, which he did study carefully when he arrived at the studio. He also studied Eisenstein and other current European masters. And he had Ford's *Stagecoach* run for him again and again, not only because it had won awards the year before but out of very high admiration for it – he put it on his list of the greatest movies of all time. He must have been influenced by all these sources. He was studying the state of the art; he was testing the water, and certainly he was girding himself to compete. And he was also Orson Welles, capable of transmuting any number of influences into something nobody had ever seen before.

The acting in *The Magnificent Ambersons* is far from the rhetoric of expressionism and farther still from the quietly and modestly inflected – almost uninflected – acting of the Hollywood style Welles would have encountered in *Stagecoach*. There is no knowing how he valued the subtly inflected performances of such a greatly intelligent mainstream Hollywood actress as Barbara Stanwyck. In contrast, the acting style of *The Magnificent Ambersons* is highly inflected, emphatic, theatrical, bold, and aggressive. Such a style may not seem an idiomatic way to record human identity on film, but in *The Magnificent Ambersons* acting must take place and be effective in dramatic scenes that are also different from ordinary scenes in Hollywood films and in the same way – more obviously and even aggressively structured, with more strongly marked beginnings, middles, and ends, and with the ends emphasized, even italicized, by clear-cut cadences. The scenes in Welles's style are organized in a blocking so exactly planned and rehearsed that it must be called choreography. Crucial dialogues take place while characters are walking with precise timing through the Amberson halls, and when these dialogues are complicated by actions of other characters, this also is done with exacting precision.

The amazing set for *The Magnificent Ambersons*, richly imagined out of a luxuriant fantasy, opulently and lovingly executed, is the natural habitat for these actors and this choreography. The centerpiece, a showpiece for both the Ambersons and the film, is the great staircase, spiraling in right angles up from the great entrance lobby, leading up to the second floor to form a wide hallway off which the Ambersons' private rooms are located, then rising to the third floor, where, following tradition, the ballroom is to be found. The staircase helps Welles organize the crowded action of the ball scene, with its many participants and the constantly changing pace and style of its movement, and he also uses the dark moodiness of the staircase and the complexity of its space to give spatial body to the tension of the dramas that take place on the second floor after the ball.

An old love revives: Eugene and Isabel, after Wilbur's death, outside the Amberson mansion. (Photo courtesy of Photofest)

The whole great set becomes charged with the conflict that constitutes the action of *The Magnificent Ambersons*.

It is on the staircase that the conflict between Fanny and George mainly takes place. Their scenes originate in actions inside rooms from which George exits with flamboyant displays of temper over his family's or the world's failure to see things his way – in particular Isabel's and Eugene's love, which he sees as a violation not only of propriety but of decency and even of moral cleanliness – the theme Tarkington took from *Hamlet*. But when George erupts from one of the these conflicts, it is to encounter Fanny, who criticizes him, or congratulates him for what he is doing ("You struck just the right treatment to adopt") – responses that are the last thing he thinks he needs; his contemptuous rejection of her reaction sets up a further conflict, which occasions new acts of insolence and rudeness.

Agnes Moorehead's impersonation of conspiratorial hysteria electrifies the whole set with overwrought hypersensitivity. She shows the Welles acting style at its most extreme, and also at its greatest, for at her high pitch she never loses subtle and delicate control. Her idiosyncratic art, which Welles praised as the best he ever worked with, looks as if it originated in ordinary observation of the inflections of ordinary people's voices and faces at moments of tension and in situations of embarrassment and stress. But Moorehead seems to distill and then compress and heighten such observations, and in doing so she fashions a concrete embodiment of the substance of Fanny's character and her life. She always works at an extreme pitch of emotion and tension, but she also obeys the values of control, continuity, and coherence. She shapes the separate moments of Fanny's behavior, the separate points she wants to make about her, into an organized and living line of action; through the extreme tension of that line she sustains attention and interest and creates the illusion that we are experiencing the whole identity of a believable human being.

After the ball, the Ambersons go to their rooms in a complex choreography that advances action and characterization, while using the key space of the second-floor hallway, beside the great stairwell, to keep the relations and conflicts focused. Isabel and George come first, discussing Wilbur's health. George is only half-concerned until his voice picks up energy at the hateful thought that his father might be investing in Eugene's automobile business. As they approach Isabel's and Wilbur's room, Wilbur himself appears at the door, a sadly anonymous apparition; at the same time Fanny and Jack enter the frame in the far background. When George again asks angrily whether his father or grandfather is financing Eugene's business, Fanny, from the background, interrupts in a high scolding tone: "You little silly. What on earth are you talking about? Eugene Morgan's perfectly able to finance his own inventions these days." Wilbur and Isabel enter their room ("I'll be in to say good-night, dear," Isabel says to George, characteristically), and George and Fanny continue arguing about Eugene, in the hallway beside the stairwell, George now suggesting that his father's unwillingness to take part in the automobile outing planned for the following day shows that he dislikes Eugene, as of course George wants him to. As he and Fanny argue, Jack emerges from his room to object to the noise they are making ("Are you two at it again?"), which George answers by another question: "What makes you and everybody so excited about this man Morgan?" Fanny's temper rises ("excited!") and she explodes in a speech that is intensified in expressivity by the interruption caused by Jack's return to his room. Her complete sentence is, "Can't people be glad to see an old friend, without silly children like you having to make a to-do about it?" But as it is actually spoken, the line is broken by Jack's exit right after her first word, which makes Fanny repeat her

"Are you two at it again?" (Collins, Moorehead, Holt). (Photo courtesy of Photofest)

"Can't" but in a higher tone and more insistently. As she and George continue walking along the hall, her voice rises still further in pitch and becomes more contorted in inflection. The originality of the sounds Moorehead makes here – she is a remarkably inventive as well as an intense artist, as in the brilliantly imagined inflection she gives that "to-do" – nevertheless keeps in touch with the tension of a realistically portrayed woman. George's voice suddenly gets excited when Fanny proposes having Eugene and Lucy to dinner, and when his opposition fires her up again, she orders him to his room with almost inarticulate choking fury. Then he changes the ground of the argument by teasing her about her own romantic interest in Eugene.

An even more stylized passage of choreographed conflict comes later in the drama, also in the great stairwell, when Jack returns after having talked with Eugene about George's having forbidden him access to the house and to Isabel. Isabel comes out eagerly to hear his news, and they both retire to the library. Then, in an unusually pronounced and explicit choreography of the camera, it shifts upward from its initial position – looking down at the library door from halfway up the staircase – to reveal that George has been observing Jack and his mother from the second-floor balcony, and when next we hear Fanny's voice, both George and the camera look up to find her taking it all in from the third-floor balcony. The spectacle of these characters monitoring each other from different levels of the staircase teeters on the brink of farce, but it is saved from the ludicrous by the precision of the choreography and the conviction of the performers. As the action moves up and down the staircase, it is exploring a space that has already been made meaningful, alive, and dramatic. When George moves down the stairs with the intent of entering the library, Fanny, with the remorseful foresight of her complex and ambivalent jealousy, rushes down to restrain him by main force from violating Isabel's suffering. Her action signals the fact that this is the moment of tragic choice for Isabel, though the choice has in fact already been made, since Isabel's submission to George has already been established as inevitable.

Fanny's next speech is one of Moorehead's greatest challenges, with its lurid melodramatic mode:

> I thought you already knew everything I did! I was just – suffering, so I wanted to let out a little. . . . Oh, I was a fool! Eugene never would have looked at me even if he'd never seen Isabel . . . and they haven't done any harm. She made Wilbur happy, and she was a true wife to him, as long as he lived. . . . And here I go, not doing myself a bit of good by it – and just ruining them.

Moorehead's job is to make serious drama out of these stagily twisting and turning revelations (closely adapted from Tarkington, however, with scarcely a word added by Welles), and she handles it, as usual, by sailing right into the wind, her voice finding for every new purpose a new color, as a great singer would, as in the choked emphasis of her operatic cry, "Oh, I was a fool!"

Agnes Moorehead's Fanny is the center of the film's theme, drama, and dramatic method. Fanny's lack of completion and fruition as lover, wife, and mother inevitably gives her an emblematic identity in this drama of fruitlessness and the failure of will – an identity strongly and clearly felt though never discussed. Her shamed sense of her own infertility generates a great anxiety that gets from the other characters patient if exasperated concern, while it places her in tacit opposition – never manifested or discussed, but continuously felt – to the quiet will-less grace of Costello's almost equally infertile Isabel.

The Magnificent Ambersons is the most tightly organized, the most fully worked, the most harmonious in style, the most richly and exactly

In the great stairwell, Fanny and George quarrel. (Photo courtesy of Photofest)

orchestrated and choreographed of all Welles's films, as the fullness and depth with which the character of Fanny is realized bears out; yet these virtues are slightly blurred in the film as we have it, which is not quite the film Welles made. It is the most excruciating irony, in a career full of ironies, that this beautifully, lovingly made film should have become, through mistakes and misjudgments on Welles's part, and through nervous commercially motivated decisions on the part of his bosses at the studio, the film most seriously damaged by Welles's bad luck in addition to his failure or refusal to learn how to work within the studio system.

The damaging of *The Magnificent Ambersons* is one of the most complicated disasters in art. Though George J. Schaefer, the head of RKO, wasn't initially enthusiastic about *Ambersons,* he eventually went along with it, only to play an equivocal role in the subsequent undermining of the film. Welles had nearly finished the shooting in February of 1942 when Schaefer proposed that he go on a mission to Latin America, which RKO had been asked to undertake by Nelson Rockefeller, who had been made the head of the new federal Office of Inter-American Affairs formed by FDR late in 1940 to improve relations between the Americas. The choice of Rockefeller was a good one, as shown in the fact that he had immediately asked Lincoln Kirstein to arrange to send an American ballet troupe to Latin America. Kirstein had been collaborating with the leading choreographer of the day, George Balanchine, in several American ballet ventures since 1933, as Rockefeller well knew. Kirstein accepted Rockefeller's invitation at once, and Balanchine just as quickly reassembled the little company he and Kirstein had recently disassembled, the American Ballet Caravan. In six weeks Balanchine composed, as showpieces for the Latin American venture, two new ballets, *Ballet Imperial* and *Concerto Barocco,* both masterpieces, which worked ideally (as his calculations always did work) for the Latin American tour and also marked a major development in Balanchine's style. It was an entirely beneficent happening. When Welles was approached with a similar suggestion, he too accepted without hesitation; it was his boss, Schaefer, after all, who had made the offer, despite the fact that *The Magnificent Ambersons* wasn't finished. What Welles was being asked to do isn't clear, but it naturally had to do with making movies, and in the end he shot thousands of feet of film stock, which, after many complications, ended up ingloriously as part of the unfinished and disorganized *It's All True.*

Welles handled capably the immediate tactical problems of going to Latin America, as might be expected from his history. He speeded up the shooting on *Ambersons* so that he could finish before leaving, working overtime himself and getting the whole company to do the same, with no apparent damage to morale. Nor is there any loss of freshness or depth of workmanship visible in the footage shot during this pressured month – Welles had been famous for crisis management on Broadway and he managed it just as easily in Hollywood. The accelerated schedule may have produced the intense concentration under which he worked best as an artist. He seemed to have handled another problem about leaving just as capably – he had fine rapport with one of his assistant directors, Robert

Wise (who had edited *Citizen Kane*), and he believed he could safely leave the editing of *Ambersons* in Wise's hands, sending instructions from Brazil by phone, telegraph, radio, or mail.

What happened to *The Magnificent Ambersons* because of Welles's absence is so important to this major film, and so painfully characteristic of Welles as a man and a professional, that it is worth detailed attention. The plans for Wise initially included having him fly down to Rio de Janeiro to work on the film there with Welles, but a sudden embargo on civilian overseas flying scotched this idea. The other arrangements didn't prove exactly impractical in themselves, though the plans for communicating by telephone, telegraph, and especially by radio do have a touch of the-world-of-the-future fantasy about them. But there is something winning about Welles's trust in the technology of long-distance communication; in this respect he wasn't actually out of touch with the realities of the world in which he was working. Hollywood people were among the first to use cross-continental air travel regularly, because of the odd setup of the industry, with the business offices in New York and the studios in Hollywood. Welles might have felt that he was living fully in his own century and in his new milieu when he proposed the idea of giving instructions electronically from Rio to his colleagues in Hollywood. The instructions did in fact get through.

Welles's plan was reasonable also because he had shot the film in the standard way, with the editing implied in the way he had written the scenes and the choices he had made about camera placement. Under these conditions, Wise edited the film competently. Then, out of the blue, Welles telegraphed a drastic revision, cutting major scenes between Isabel and George, ordering a new scene shot – nobody has figured out what this was all about. But though Wise received the order just before the first preview in Pomona, he had time to make the changes Welles asked for, even to the point of shooting the new scene.

The disastrous results of the Pomona preview have become legendary – most of the audience reported on their little cards that they found the movie dark, boring, dull, dreary. Such previews mattered a lot to the studios; though Darryl Zanuck had in a famous instance disregarded the negative responses at a preview of *The Grapes of Wrath,* and had been proved right by the great artistic and commercial success of that film, this is almost the only exception to the rule. To most studio heads it would have seemed almost crazy to go ahead with projects that previews predicted would bore or offend the public. It was also standard practice to try to "fix" movies that had got bad responses. Schaefer himself attended the Pomona preview, and was devastated, understandably, for it was at his behest that RKO had invested a million dollars in the film (way over budget, and a lot of money in those days), and he had invested his own professional reputation in Welles. According to Robert L. Carringer's *"The Magnificent Ambersons": A Reconstruction,* Wise and his colleagues guessed immediately that it was Welles's huge cut that was at fault, since by sapping the emotional life in the relation between Isabel and her son, it had indeed made the film seem dreary; when they substantially restored the original version, and ran another preview in Pasadena, they got a much more favorable result.[2] But this version was still too long; length had always been a worry, for Welles's 131-minute film was outside the Hollywood norm, and it's conceivable that Welles was trying to handle the problem of length by his cut. By now Schaefer was getting nervous about the whole enterprise, partly perhaps because of the unrealistic recklessness of Welles's big revision. He drifted this way and that, trying to decide what to do, and finally, since he had the right to cut the film (as confirmed by the company lawyer, whom he carefully consulted), he did cut it, and on a large scale. Now, following standard practice in such matters, Schaefer ordered many small cuts in Welles's original, which added up to a large cut of forty-three minutes, and he ordered the two final scenes replaced with new scenes shot by Freddie Fleck and cast in a more upbeat mood than Welles's version, which had notably avoided such sentimentality. And then Fleck went one better, in a failure hard to credit in an experienced professional, by shooting the new scenes clumsily and in a style and tone that didn't match Welles's.

We will never know exactly how much the power, meaning, and atmosphere of *The Magnificent Ambersons* were damaged by what the studio did, since Welles's original was destroyed shortly afterward, and the studio cut is the version we all know and the only one that now exists. But the continuity cutting script rediscovered and reprinted by Carringer tells us the content and dialogue of the cut scenes, so that we may with some confidence guess how badly the film was damaged.

The oddest cut is of a short scene in which young George Minafer forcibly resumes control over his club when he returns from college. From the dialogue it is hard to make out how the scene could have worked, dependent as it is on youthful actors with whom we aren't familiar, but since Welles rarely attempted anything he didn't know how to do, the chances are that we lost something interesting. Most of the lost scenes, though, are continuations or variations of material already presented and rather fully developed. On the page of the complete script, these scenes are full of interesting and vivid detail, and they don't seem damagingly repetitive, for the tone and method of the film as it stands encourages the slow development of its meanings and feelings – *The Magnificent Ambersons* is, to say the least, not an action film. On the other hand, Schaefer's commercial reason for cutting these scenes – that the film had seemed too long for many of the spectators at the previews – doesn't on the face of it seem outrageously stupid or philistine, and it is perfectly conceivable that cutting these somewhat repetitive scenes did no serious harm to the feel of the film, which, as it stands, in the drastically cut version we all know, seems to capture richly the melancholy and lovingly slow movement that Welles must have intended. If one puts oneself into the practical minds at RKO, one can see them as having done a sensible and even a not-insensitive job.

Conceivably a more important cut was made in a spectacular technical achievement in the ballroom scene. As Welles tells Bogdanovich, they cut "twenty seconds playing time and cut into two pieces our crane shot that would have played for a whole reel without a cut."[3] His point is how ridiculously small a gain in time the studio achieved by this cut, weighed against the beauty and power, and the virtuosity, of the effect of the whole scene photographed without a cut. One takes Welles's word that "a whole reel without a cut" would have been something marvelous – he had achieved enough marvels in other scenes to deserve our trust.

Looking at the cutting script, I myself don't find the loss of most of those forty-three minutes very upsetting, partly because some of the cut passages repeat points already made, and partly because some would have been cut in any case. From the moment Welles finished the film at 131 minutes, Schaefer was certain to start demanding cuts, which Welles was legally powerless to stop and which he might well have gone along with, wunderkind genius or no; he was a tough professional, unlikely to cave in at the idea of cutting his own work. As far as I can judge, no major meaning, or feeling, or atmosphere was lost in this huge cut.

The additional footage shot by Fleck is another matter. The glaring discrepancies in technique and texture between Welles's original and Fleck's additions are hard to believe. Wise was in charge of the overall project; giving him the assignment must have seemed a good idea, for he was certified loyal to Welles, and Welles had left the film in his care. But it was not a good idea, since he seems to have had no problem with Fleck's additional material. It goes without saying that Fleck's scenes would be inferior to Welles's, but that they should be so bafflingly inconsistent with

Welles's in elementary matters of style remains impossible to explain. The short next-to-last scene, in which Lucy and Eugene decide to go to see George in the hospital after he has been badly injured by an automobile, is unnecessary and clumsily out of place in Welles's elliptical narrative method; but the argument must have been that people at the previews and at the studio had complained that they couldn't always follow what was happening, and literal-minded viewers might not understand that Eugene and Lucy had been visiting George unless they saw them decide to do so. But granted its necessity, the scene itself jolts our attention by having absolutely nothing of Welles's signature look in terms of lighting, fluent interaction of the characters, placement of the camera – matters of style that Wise had to have seen Welles arranging at every point of the filming. Fleck seems even to have inhibited the brilliant Joseph Cotten and Anne Baxter into clumsy ineffectuality.

The final scene is worse. That it looks utterly unlike Welles is the least of the problems. Welles's screenplay was rewritten in frank disobedience to his intention. In Fleck's version, we see Eugene and Fanny walking down the hospital corridor, having just visited George; Lucy is still with George, and a rapprochement is in process. As they move toward us, borne on heavenly music, Eugene confides to Fanny: "You know something, Fanny? I wouldn't tell this to anybody but you. But it seemed to me as if someone else was in that room, and that through me she brought her boy under shelter again, and that I'd been true at last to my true love." Fanny welcomes this with a radiant smile. The final scene as Welles planned it also contains this fantasy (which comes from Tarkington), but with one immense difference – Eugene tells it, as some surviving stills of the lost sequence show, in a bleak boardinghouse to an almost unresponsive Fanny; the continuity script tells us that Fanny rocks in a squeaking rocking chair all the way through the scene, and at times she is so far out of touch with Eugene that she doesn't even know whom he is talking about. Welles's intention here is intelligently tough, painful, and moving. The lack of sympathy between these two people who have gone through their lives together is a hard irony that isn't in the novel and clearly came from Welles's own invention. So painfully dark a view of the end of the Ambersons may have disappointed an audience's need for a happy ending, and disappointed the worried Schaefer's need too, but Welles's ending, so rich in understanding of character, is exact and right, because it fits everything else in the film, and because it even fits Tarkington's novel better than Tarkington's own ending. That Eugene should be making a fool of himself by being so out of touch with Fanny's mood may have seemed hard for an audience to comprehend, but Cotten's large, warm presence would have carried it off. Welles wanted to preserve Tarkington's final fantasy, but he also wanted to shape it into a darker and more realistic – and far more original and interesting – configuration of all the elements in Tarkington's situation.

The loss of Welles's ending is one of the great calamities in filmmaking. It's hard to decide whether anybody is to blame and, if so, who. It's not true, as many believe, that Welles fecklessly abandoned *Ambersons* when a more interesting offer came along. He thought continually about *Ambersons* while he was in Brazil, and (in addition to the puzzling cut he proposed) he came up with a multitude of suggestions – all this is on record. By means of his elaborate plan of communication, he was consulted about every decision Schaefer made, and he responded to them all, sometimes with a concession, more often of course with long explanations why the proposed changes were wrong. Abstractly speaking, he was even involved in the process of cutting those forty-three minutes and perhaps (this correspondence has been lost), even had something to do with reshooting the ending. But in practice, thinking about *Ambersons* in Brazil, being told what was happening and reporting his thoughts in long telegrams and telephone calls, wasn't in the least the same thing as being right on the scene in Hollywood, a powerful intellectual and physical presence, explaining and contesting, in the room where the decisions were being made. Though he might not in the end have carried the day in arguing with Schaefer for his choices, it is hard to believe that his powerful gift for persuasion would not have made a difference. But of course he wasn't physically on the scene – that is the long and the short of it. And, however sound, reasonable, or even politically crucial FDR's purpose in the Latin American venture was, in hindsight it's obvious that Welles should have turned it down – it put into unreasonable jeopardy his professional life in the movies, which, despite his fame, was still in its early phases.

And yet, and yet – hindsight also tells us how inconceivable turning the offer down would have seemed in 1942 to this intense admirer of FDR's. So Welles accepted the offer, and suddenly he had a far greater problem on his hands than he thought. If he counted a lot on the luck and energy that went with his youth and his sense of brilliant accomplishment, they let him down. Getting *Ambersons* edited correctly in the circumstances that prevailed was perhaps insoluble even for this magician.

Yet *The Magnificent Ambersons* as we have it, with all its cuts and glaringly inappropriate additions, doesn't stay in the mind as an incomplete or damaged work. In our memories, what Welles and his players created eclipses Wise's mistakes – and that happens even when we watch the film again, egregious as the flaws seem when we're concentrating on them. Selective attention and selective remembering happen all the time in art – mercifully, or we'd always be letting flaws ruin our pleasure in all the art we love.

4

The Lady from Shanghai

In the midforties Welles was active on many projects in many places. He worked hard for Roosevelt's 1944 campaign while continuing his own political writing. In drama and film he interested himself in non-dramatic forms that might change the experience of going to the theater or to the movies. With the same purpose he tried to get backing for *It's All True,* and to find a more effective shape for this anomalous pet project, composed of a little story called "Bonito the Bull," a documentary about jazz, and some of the footage he had shot in Latin America for the Rockefeller project. He made a half-joking "contribution to the war effort" in *The Mercury Wonder Show,* a ninety-minute magic show performed in a tent on Cahuenga Boulevard in Hollywood, right next to the big official USO, late in the summer of 1943. It was a one-man show, but Welles had taught friends some simple tricks – Joseph Cotten had an assignment. Welles inevitably performed the world's most famous trick, that of sawing a woman in half. The first subject was his latest love, soon to be his wife, Rita Hayworth; but Harry Cohn, her boss at Columbia, wouldn't let his supervaluable star devalue herself, and he made her quit. She was replaced to great effect by an old friend of Welles's, Marlene Dietrich.

The more ambitious project of *Around the World in Eighty Days* occupied Welles for many months. After Mike Todd withdrew financial backing (he was later to produce a star-studded Technicolor film version [1956]), Welles was left with the immediate practical problem of large debts, and he now initiated what would be the pattern of his financial career from that point on: using whatever money he was earning in a current project to repay debts contracted in past projects, only to contract new debts in the new project.

To pay these debts, and also out of personal taste and conviction, Welles carried on his customary activities in radio and in left-liberal political commentary during and immediately after the war, and he also directed and acted in two films: the un-Wellesian *The Stranger,* made for International Pictures and released in 1946, and the extremely Wellesian *The Lady from Shanghai,* made for Columbia and released in 1948 – both done to fulfill contractual and financial obligations, neither derived from material of much importance to him personally. The producer William Goetz, who had been at Twentieth Century–Fox when Welles had acted in *Jane Eyre* there in 1943, had been sufficiently impressed by Welles to want to use him when he got a production setup of his own; when he founded International Pictures, he followed through on his promise and produced *The Stranger.* He must have been impressed also with Welles's reputation for never finishing films, for he drew up a contract that put Welles under severe restraints, which Welles seems actually to have welcomed. *The Lady from Shanghai* originated as a way of paying off the debt of $25,000 he had contracted with Harry Cohn, the head of Columbia Pictures, to help finance his staged *Around the World; Lady from Shanghai* was the only film Welles made with Rita Hayworth, the big star at Columbia, to whom he had been married and from whom he was now getting divorced.

The Stranger has been generally condescended to, mostly because it deserves to be, partly because Welles, perhaps taking his cue from the restrictions of his contract with Goetz, spoke of it repeatedly as his one solid, reasonable, sane, ordinary, conventional film, the proof that he could deliver the everyday virtues of moviemaking as well as the brilliant feats of virtuosity for which he was better known. And apart from a few Wellesian camera setups and depth shots, *The Stranger* is decidedly conventional, if not entirely unsuccessfully so, as in Welles's own performance. He plays Franz Kindler, an escaped Nazi, formerly high in the Nazi hierarchy and the self-styled creator of the Final Solution; he is hiding out after the war, waiting for the Nazis to come to power again, in a picture-postcard Connecticut town, disguised as a prep-school teacher named Charles Rankin; he is newly married for love to a proper judge's daughter. Welles's performance sees the passion, even the idealism of this man, and he makes clear the way these elements intersect with the megalomania of his beliefs. If his performance never suggests a degree of inhumanity commensurate with our current conception of the Final Solution, that insufficiency probably shows how little was known about the camps and their true purpose right after the war. Edward G. Robinson as Inspector Wilson, on the trail of Kindler, plays with his usual intelligent craft and his knack of giving a moral and spiritual dimension to the hunt he is conducting; yet one has to agree with what Welles said to Bogdanovich, "I think Robinson is one of the best movie actors of all time, but I thought it was too obvious casting."[1] Loretta Young, as the new wife, Mary Longstreet, is competently professional, though a bit weak and faded. Welles plays convincingly as her husband. The action, non-Wellesian in its linearity, moves strongly toward its satisfactory climax. Some rather fancy symbolism at the finale – Kindler dies in a kind of suicide, impaled on the sword of a mechanical knightly figure revolving around the church clock with which he loves to tinker – has been carefully prepared for and is executed with tact. All in all, this is the responsible professionalism Welles said he aimed for.

But *The Stranger* isn't very interesting and doesn't matter very much, particularly to people who value Welles's work highly. Its main interest may lie in showing how oddly characterless an artist Welles became when making what seemed to him a vernacular film – he tried to talk himself into it, but vernacular moviemaking wasn't in his repertory.

The brilliant and overwrought *The Lady from Shanghai* is well within Welles's repertory, and means more to his admirers than *The Stranger*, if for less dignified reasons – it didn't propose to be and certainly didn't turn out to be conventional or well-mannered, and in fact it's the most overheated film Welles directed. I've vacillated widely about it over the years; I've implicated it too often in the ups and downs of my own taste and judgment to offer a fully disinterested estimate even now. When first I saw it, in 1948, *The Lady from Shanghai* became a kind of addiction. I wanted to experience its atmosphere and wit, its flamboyant style, again and again; Welles seemed to be aiming for a new record in bravura, in gratuitous brilliance and perversity, and that was fine with me. My pleasure in this art of excess felt like an exciting private discovery: *The Lady from Shanghai* seemed crafted expressly to suit people like me. The ripest and most lurid elements were the ones I loved best: pulpy, sweaty Glenn Anders as George Grisby, in tight close-up, along with the preposterously empty innuendo with which he voices his crazed proposition to Michael O'Hara, the Welles figure: "I want you to kiiiill me!" Or his juicy sexual salute to the illicit lovers after he has caught them alone on the yacht, "So long, kiddies. . . . Bye-bye."

I loved everything about the character Arthur Bannister, played by Everett Sloane. Something Welles said to Bogdanovich about Sloane in *This Is Orson Welles* catches the mode *of The Lady from Shanghai:*

BOGDANOVICH: Why did you cripple Bannister so completely – both legs?
WELLES: Because Everett Sloane was basically a radio actor; he'd never really learned to *move*. He was like a marionette. That was OK for Bernstein in *Kane*. But it didn't seem to me that a marionette would be a great criminal lawyer. So I made him an elaborate sort of cripple. And of course he loved it. All actors like to play cripples.[2]

The casual use of "cripple" (now out of bounds) suits the high spirits of the discussion ('Glad you asked,' Welles's volubility seems to say); and Welles captures the flair of Sloane's brilliant performance. When Sloane first appears in the seamen's hiring hall, the camera is fascinated by his immovable legs and the canelike crutches he uses to propel himself forward; in the night scene on the yacht, heavy with unfulfilled and perverse yearnings, we imagine Bannister's crutches more vividly because we don't see him at all – we only hear his grating false tone to his wife, of whose liaison with O'Hara he is self-hatingly, even gloatingly aware; when he mounts his world's-greatest-lawyer stunt of cross-examining himself during the trial, the crutches italicize the insolence of his approach to the witness box; and in the finale, the crutches really come into their own when they are first caught by the light as they precede Bannister, then multiplied endlessly in the mirrors of the funhouse. Welles's patronizing tone about Sloane seems wrong, for Sloane seems to know Welles's maxim, "All actors like to play cripples," as well as Welles does, and he sails right into its implications. And we, the audience for Sloane's self-performing, self-delighting art, cooperate with the huge tastelessness of those crutches without compunction, exempt as we are from judgment by knowing exactly what we are doing. We are all in it together, playing our assigned roles in this self-performing theatrical art, in the Welles Theater, and enjoying *The Lady from Shanghai* in particular because it's more playful in its excess than Welles's other performative and theatrical films.

Fifty-odd years later my response to all this has somewhat dimmed. When *The Lady from Shanghai* came out in 1948, some years had passed since my first experience of *The Magnificent Ambersons* in 1942 and of *Citizen Kane* in 1943, yet my excitement about them hadn't dwindled in the least. I was still an eager devotee of the Welles Theater of self-performance; I felt intense curiosity about what the great performer would offer in this new film, and my pleasure in Welles's presence behind *The Lady from Shanghai* was as strong as I expected it to be. That pleasure is diminished now, and my sense of Welles's presence is intermittent and sometimes a bit irritated rather than welcoming.

Bannister (Everett Sloane) approaches the witness box, where he is going to cross-examine himself. O'Hara (Welles), the man on trial, sits at right. (Photo courtesy of Photofest)

The Lady from Shanghai was adapted from Sherwood King's *If I Die before I Wake,* a novel just a shade more dignified than pulp fiction. Like other such novels on which many films of the late forties were based, King's is a variation on clichés of crime and betrayal. Important films were based on this dubious material in the forties and fifties, including some major works of film art, and in the late fifties French film critics studied the whole phenomenon seriously, giving it the name "film noir."[3] Since this term is now used indiscriminately to refer to the dark films of crime and violence that began to be made during the war, it has acquired an agenda of cultural history rather than being used simply to describe films accurately or to make clear distinctions among them. The agenda is a crudely melodramatic version of American culture after World War II, which sees all postwar crime, violence, and betrayal films as caused by and representing postwar American disillusion, despair, alienation, or nihilism, due variously to postwar fatigue, McCarthyism, or the bomb.

The Lady from Shanghai, which contains plenty of violence and betrayal, despair and nihilism, has been gathered into this category and into this historical meaning.

When I first got addicted to *The Lady from Shanghai* in 1948, well before the polularization of the term "film noir," I had already also seen many of the films now identified as "noir," but I didn't find this political meaning in them, nor did I really group them all together; nor did I connect Welles's film with them. Perhaps I was naïvely unaware of the implications of the films I was enjoying one by one. But I did connect *The Lady from Shanghai* with the Welles films I already knew, and the things about it I paid attention to were the elements of the Welles flamboyant style I recognized and loved. And this still seems the right connection to have made. I valued other crime films, several of them very highly, some more highly than *The Lady from Shanghai,* but they occupied a different part of my mind. I regarded *The Lady from Shanghai* and still do as a work of self-conscious extravagance – moving exotic people through exotic settings, and involving them all in an almost indecipherable intrigue. But in the crime films of the forties that interested me, crime, betrayal – "trouble" – happened in the ordinary, everyday life of ordinary people. These films recorded the look of everyday American people and landscapes in an attentive and respectful way that I much admired, and I admired too the quietness of the filmmaking that went along with that realism – for it made its record seem true.

A modest example is the 1948 B-film *Pitfall,* directed by André de Toth, in which the agent of violence and betrayal, Mona Stevens (Lizabeth Scott), damages and almost destroys the everyday ordinariness of the married life of John and Sue Forbes (Dick Powell and Jane Wyatt). Their marriage is strained and weary, as it happens, and the film records this dispassionately, but with considerable attention and curiosity. *Pitfall* is imitative and derivative but not the less interesting for that, because it is also interested in being accurate about its subject. De Toth's debt to other films makes the identity of his own film easy to catch, and makes such a comparison an absorbing endeavor, as it was for all of us who followed these films in the forties. Everybody in *Pitfall* is life size, the film itself is life size; house, work, family, all are routine, ordinary, humdrum, unlikely materials for drama. The disruptive force is herself curiously life size. Lizabeth Scott had been being promoted as potential star material for several years before *Pitfall,* but without much success, and her talents were decidedly limited. What de Toth uses, to great effect, is not her actuality as a star but those characteristics that led to her being considered for stardom in the first place – the mystery and sexual suggestiveness in her breathy voice – which gives a special trademark to the routine Hollywood glamour of her appearance; de Toth locates something incomplete in her that makes her ordinary while continuing to hold promise of something out of the ordinary. The result is that Lizabeth Scott's power seems just the right size and intensity for the ordinary life she disrupts; an image neither cheap nor fake, but close to both. It is this unachieved promise and potential to which Dick Powell's John Forbes is attracted and into which he pours his fantasies of escape.

Tourneur's *Out of the Past* (1947), by common consent the paradigm for the crime and betrayal film of the period and perhaps its masterpiece, complicates the pattern by making the hero, Jeff Markham (Robert Mitchum), not so much an ordinary man as a man hiding out in ordinariness from a world of violence and betrayal, in which he was not only involved but played a leading part. He is very much an equivocal figure morally, and his position in his new world of the everyday is precarious; the film takes his measure in these respects with subtle sympathy. His rediscovery by Joe Stefanos (Paul Valentine), an agent of the violence of the past, sets the film in motion. It leads Jeff to a tormented and intensely self-hating recapitulation of the acts and feelings of his earlier life, and in the end leads him to kill the betraying woman, Kathie (Jane Greer), and to join her in a weary, despairing suicidal death, aligning himself with the corruption to which he believes he belongs by nature.

Jeff is fishing in a pastoral stream when Joe comes up out of the past; the image of ordinary life in these films often takes the form of such banal stereotypes. The whole presentation of the ordinary life in which Jeff is hiding out and hoping to find happiness mixes suggestiveness with clumsy cliché. The girl he loves in the ordinary world, Ann (Virginia Huston), is a paragon of neat, blonde, middle-class respectability – pretty hard to take; but she rebels against that tight identity by falling in love with Jeff and remaining loyal to him against the by no means easily discounted will of her suspicious and disapproving father and mother. Her loyalty to Jeff costs her something, since Mitchum is glaringly out of place in this ordinary world, threatening to its values in every aspect of his behavior, and in every aspect of his sheer physicality, the way he carries himself, his instinctive body-certainty, his almost insolent slowness. But Ann's admirable courage tends to express itself in awful little lectures about the good in everybody and other Sunday-school material. The film's ambiguity about the value of Ann's small-town goodness may in part be due to ineptitude or to carelessness in casting, directing, and acting, yet this ambiguous performance does succeed in carrying its weight in the value system of the film, for it sharpens the focus on the dangerously protean Kathie, on whose power to charm and betray the action depends.

Ordinariness takes many forms in these films – their wide range of tone was a factor in their popularity and usefulness to the studios. In *Double Indemnity*, it is the Barbara Stanwyck character herself (Phyllis Dietrichson), whose deadly purposefulness invites violent crime into her life and house, and into the life of her casual lover, Walter Neff (Fred MacMurray). In this film the ordinary life isn't the object of respectful attention; it is a cheap life, house, husband, and world that she wants to escape. Much of the power of the film comes from the hypnotic fascination with which we follow Dietrichson's actions and understand her motives, and also from the cold clarity and contempt with which the director, Billy Wilder, observes and asks us to observe these events, with the brilliant Stanwyck as his perfect instrument.

In contrast, Max Ophuls (another German émigré director, like Wilder) brings to *The Reckless Moment* not only something of Wilder's accurately detailed knowledge of everyday American domestic life – it's hard to imagine where and how he and Wilder picked it up – but a delicate sympathy with the film's extraordinarily original subject: the fantastically rigorous demands of American everyday domestic life. The dimension of this life comes to our attention, admiration, and almost our awe through the superb collaboration between Ophuls and Joan Bennett in building this character, the all-capable, deeply ordinary, extremely decent, and very tense Lucia Harper; her submission to what is expected of her requires her to handle entirely on her own all the consequences of her daughter's crime, some of them involving extreme physical endurance. *The Reckless Moment* is both celebration and critique of this state of affairs: admiring the strength – of mind and spirit and also, amazingly, of body – that American culture asks of this ordinary well-fixed middle-class woman when trouble threatens a member of her family, and just as clearly showing the terrible cost of this almost compulsive sense of responsibility in Mrs. Harper's unremitting tension, her almost mechanical sense of connection with the family she is going to such lengths to protect, and in her own locked-in emotional life. The complexity of this character is balanced by what would generically be the figure of threat and disruption, Martin Donnelly (the James Mason character), for he is himself a victim fronting under compulsion for the real threat, and his capacity for imaginative, eventually loving observation gives him insight into the strain and courage of Mrs. Harper's life – love and insight that almost but not quite touch her into the awakened emotional expressivity that might lead her out of her box of duty.

In *The Big Sleep* Howard Hawks endows Bogart and Bacall with what might oxymoronically be called his own special ordinariness, a casually elegant and knowing way of taking life, informed with a sense of style that creates a whole civilization that is threatened but not finally corrupted by the sleaziness and violence surrounding the Sternwood family; part of the power of the film arises from this consonance between maker and material.

Several films from 1944–50 – *Criss Cross, Cry of the City, The Killers, Christmas Holiday, The File on Thelma Jordon* – are the work of my favorite of these directors, Robert Siodmak, though it was only later that I realized that these unassuming crime films added up to make him a master director – in particular in his reports of the look and behavior of ordinary Americans and their surroundings. The scene in which Steve (Burt Lancaster) and Anna (Yvonne de Carlo) meet in the drugstore in *Criss Cross* has remained my touchstone for what accuracy of perception – physical and moral – in rendering the whole envelope of particulars of American behavior and culture looks like. Siodmak's record has the dispassionate clarity and authority of the findings of anthropology, but makes no such claims.

Taking ordinary everyday life as their subject was an intelligent choice for these directors to have made, and a smart choice for their financial bosses to have gone along with – it made for interesting films. But it did more; it allowed and even obliged the directors and actors of the movies – superb artists working with the modesty of craftsmen – to capitalize on and explore the basic realism of the film medium, film's idiomatic alliance with the surface of reality. And that alliance with film's essence, which led to modesty in the moviemaking of these directors, gave them a blessed exemption from Hollywood's normally inflated packaging of American themes and celebration of American values, and released their writers, directors, and actors into fresh observation of our culture.

I discovered the films of Siodmak, Tourneur, Wilder, Ford, and Hawks at the same time as I was discovering the classic realistic still photography of Walker Evans, Dorothea Lange, and their colleagues – I don't know which came first. What I remember as the first time I saw the power and beauty of this mode of rendering reality is the opening of John Ford's *The Grapes of Wrath* in 1940 – a steady and insistent tracking of the concrete highway along which Tom Joad is on his way home from prison. The focus on the divider line in the highway and on the multitude of oil stains made those images inexplicably important and meaningful in the same way that the great documentary still photographs of Evans and the others are meaningful – because they are recording the surface of reality with skill and clarity, without rhetoric, sentimentality, or political agenda. I felt I was watching as if in revelation a representation of the life around me. This connection between the crime films of the late forties and the medium of realistic photography helps explain why Americans didn't tire soon of a genre that had such fertility. The longevity of the genre certainly also owed a lot to the thrill of the material itself, the drama of crime and betrayal that I am perhaps scanting; but somewhere in their power over us lies the power of representation itself. Representation is a fact of everybody's daily life and offers a value and a pleasure that we forget about at the cost of dehumanization.

I was implicated in an entertaining, perhaps sad, example of the power of representation some years ago in the Metropolitan Museum of Art in New York. I was hunting for the newly acquired Greek vase by the great maker Euphronius, already scandalously famous because the Met may have acquired it in equivocal circumstances that amounted to bootlegging. Whether or not it had been robbed from its proper owners in Italy, or from Italy itself, it was destined to be famous both for its beauty and for its size. When I finally located the room in which it was on display, I admired first the theatrical lighting that turned an ordinary room in the museum into a shrine hushed for the veneration of the sacred object; I admired the size of the vase, of course, and in due course I admired the vase itself, and then the painting on it. Then I found something else to admire. On the walls of the shrine had been installed gigantic enlargements of black-and-white photographs of the vase; once discovered, they were irresistibly attractive, unsettlingly so, and I discovered that their power was working on the other people in the room, who, after paying their respects to the Euphronius vase, as I did, then paid what seemed really serious attention to the photographs. The irony was deafening – here was *the very object, the thing itself,* in a room expressly and very skillfully designed to show it off; yet all of us were engrossed in looking at these representations rather than the reality. You might claim that you could see the details of the vase painting better in the photographs because the enlargements were so alluringly large; but this was the big, the huge, Euphronius vase, the figures on which couldn't have been easier to see, and the vase was accommodatingly placed at eye level. Moreover, the coloring of the vase gave the figures a different kind of legibility from that of the photographs, and study showed that it was a better, a greater kind. But it was clear that the pleasure all of us were taking in the representation was different from that of looking at the real vase. And better – that's where the crowd was.

The Lady from Shanghai almost entirely lacks interest in and respect for the surface of everyday reality. Instead of recording the lives of ordinary Americans, it deals with bizarre, grotesque, sinister people who inhabit a world governed by fantastic intrigue. Most of the film takes place in exotic settings. The whole style and look of the film seems geared to lead up to the notably memorable finale in a funhouse hall of mirrors. Steve and Anna in *Criss Cross* meet in a drugstore, Phyllis and Walter in *Double Indemnity* meet in a supermarket, but Michael and Elsa meet for a tryst in an aquarium, in front of great tanks of fish swimming slowly about behind them; they hide from pursuit in San Francisco's Chinatown, where Elsa electrifyingly begins to ask directions in fluent Chinese, and then in a Chinese theater, in the middle of a performance, the oddity of which we hear and see from every possible angle. Their meeting at the opening of the film, in Central Park at night, has a luxurious, sumptuous look, with Elsa gleaming in white against velvety blackness, her glamorous beauty seeming both expensively remote and teasingly accessible. The yacht reeks of luxury and exclusion, as do all the grand-tour ports of call, where we climb steep hills from the port to get spectacular views of famous bays or mountains, and get to go on a huge picnic through swamps and through slow romantic parades of hundreds of lit up boats at night. In *The Lady from Shanghai* subtle observation of the particulars of American life as it is actually lived seems to be of no interest to any of the participants – writer, director, actor, or cinematographer.

The glamour of the locations is matched by the eccentricity of the personnel. Bannister's crutches are indicative of his impotence and of his brilliantly successful way of triumphing over it. The glamorous halting places in the voyage are again and again infected by Grisby's not quite sane, obsessed exposition of his murder proposition to Michael. The proposition in itself is utterly remote from the crimes people actually commit and the way they commit them.

The overdone oddity of people and places in the film is confirmed by default when, after the killings in the funhouse, Michael escapes into what the film presents as the real world. This is not the real urban world as in a film by Siodmak or Wilder, but an italicized ordinariness: a luridly lifeless and featureless cold gray morning light on the drab deserted structures of the funhouse, empty streets, desolate and apparently abandoned buildings – all photographed with a superbly engineered hyped-up variation of the tonality of ordinary film and still-photograph documentary.

The gritty streets in *The Magnificent Ambersons* – which Welles drew from the same sources of still photography as in this passage at the end of *The Lady from Shanghai* – were bleakly ordinary, but they were alive with a drama in which we too had been involved, the streets of a town we had come to know, which we see as the deflated young George sees them as he walks through them, as if for the first time: The nature of depression the streets make him feel is exact, and we know where it comes from.

That *The Lady from Shanghai* doesn't belong in the category of films that follow the standards of realism set up by Siodmak, Tourneur, Wilder, and the rest is hardly surprising. *The Lady from Shanghai* is a "performance" of a crime and betrayal film such as we should expect from that performing artist, Orson Welles. And much of it works brilliantly well.

Rita Hayworth, as the deceitful Elsa Bannister, at many key junctures embodies the conventional ambiguity of the character with quiet originality. She is wonderful in the opening – we spot her at once as the dangerous woman, but the unexpected simple niceness of her behavior complicates things, and the way she holds steady the ambiguity about what she is up to is the main force that keeps the film in focus. In the opening episode Elsa's smiling cool friendliness, and the elegance with which she holds herself relaxed and poised in the carriage, are intensified by Hayworth's beauty and by our awareness that the expensive sumptuousness with which she is photographed is somebody's tribute to her beauty and power.

At the opposite end of the scale, Welles's performance as the solid, decent man betrayed by this deceitful woman is so ineffective as to damage the film irreparably. The character is Michael O'Hara, a sailor-drifter-poet-political activist who encounters Elsa Bannister riding alone in a carriage in Central Park, falls under her spell immediately, and rescues her when she is attacked by thieves. He is sought out the following day in the seamen's hiring hall, at Elsa's suggestion, by her husband, the famous, brilliant, crippled criminal lawyer Arthur Bannister, whose impotence is insinuated glancingly and who we realize is in some fashion pandering for his wife. Bannister hires O'Hara as a hand on their upcoming voyage by yacht from New York to San Francisco, during which O'Hara inevitably becomes embroiled not only in a liaison with Elsa but also in other perverse machinations of the Bannister world, notably a crazy scheme of Bannister's partner, George Grisby, in which O'Hara will pretend to kill Grisby in a scheme to get insurance money, which Grisby will then spend in a paradise in the South Seas. In the end it is predictably Elsa who has been

"Somebody's tribute to her beauty and power": Elsa (Rita Hayworth) with O'Hara at the funhouse entrance. (Photo courtesy of Photofest)

the source of the plotting (though the film is so cryptically and elliptically made that, at many points, it is not secure plot information but only our sense of the habits of the genre that helps us realize what is going on and distinguish the good from the bad); O'Hara meets her and Bannister for a shoot-out in a funhouse hall of mirrors and barely escapes after the spouses kill each other.

The conventional requirements for a role like O'Hara's are solid, easy strength and extreme sexual vulnerability – neither of which Welles was good at conveying. It is well known that he had the fighting in the opening scene performed by stunt men, but that is of no consequence, and his actual size is fine; the impression the camera takes of Welles in this role is that he lacks centered solidity. Likewise, though Welles himself was an inexhaustible womanizer, he doesn't project the appearance of that identity. O'Hara's behavior with Elsa, even in the clinches, is thickly inexpressive; after the opening scene, he never looks stirred by Hayworth's beauty. He was, it is true, performing a romantic role opposite the woman to whom he had been married and from whom he was estranged, and what we're seeing is perhaps overconfidence about his ability to mask his uneasiness in the situation; but one guesses rather, from this as well as other films, that the appearance of romantic passion was not in his repertory.

The image of the ordinary man deceived by the dangerous woman was one Hollywood was well equipped to supply. Having the physique and temperament for such roles was the requirement, but these were not very stringent restrictions, for the roles could be played effectively by many physical and temperamental types and in many styles and tones. The anchor of *Out of the Past* in terms both of plot and temperament is the solid presence of Robert Mitchum, one of the standbys in this sort of film, who only later emerged in the histories as a major actor of the period. He is the kind of actor whom unobservant people like to describe as "always the same," as are many Hollywood actors; but it takes little practice in looking to see that Mitchum was actually master of a great range of tones in which he subtly conveyed a great range of identities and experiences, particularly moral experiences. The key images of the ordinary man betrayed by the dishonest and deceitful woman could be varied endlessly by regulating the tonal values of either character – making the woman more or less sinister in surface behavior, the man more or less obtuse or brutal – variations that refreshed stereotypes while efficiently manipulating audience expectations. The "always the same" quality in these actors, particularly the men, made them good at representing the ordinary and also made them available to the camera. Not projecting a highly pronounced or idiosyncratic identity, they became a neutral ground on which emotions and attitudes and tones could be recorded with the quiet subtlety necessary for successful transfer to the tremendous enlargement of the big screen. Hollywood at this moment was lucky in having at hand a large supply of leading men and women who were also able to suggest in particular the experience of mature emotional life.

All of this matters because *The Lady from Shanghai* is seriously lacking in forward-moving continuity, and that continuity would conventionally have been provided by an actor who would hold the film together by the power and conviction with which he could represent sexual longing. *The*

Lady from Shanghai is structurally weak in other ways. The yacht's voyage has no legible shape, and the sense that it is touching on a wide range of locale is shallow. Our curiosity about Grisby's plot carries the film for a while, but the plot is too bizarre and too obscure to sustain interest once we know what it involves, and not the least attempt is made to amplify its hold on the audience's imagination – this whole element of the film disappears into a mystification that isn't tantalizing and enlivening but irritating.

Perhaps Welles's trouble with this role lay in his playing it too quietly. In the hiring hall, when Bannister asks for O'Hara, the latter's friend Goldie (Gus Schilling) calls him "Black Irish," and that caricature name suggests a much more vivid impersonation than what Welles delivers. Other elements support this. The first thing we encounter in the film, and hear throughout in a voice-over narrative, is O'Hara's heavy brogue. It is unconvincing and inept and an obvious mistake, yet one can imagine a more emphatic version of this impersonation forming a strong part of an entire conception. It looks like pigheadedness – Welles's stubborn refusal not to cast himself in a role he couldn't pull off – but it may have been simply a miscalculation.

5

Touch of Evil

Shortly after Welles began shooting *Touch of Evil* in 1957 he enlisted Marlene Dietrich in the project.

> "Oh she's marvelous!" says Orson of her performance. "It's her last great role. She was such a wonderful soldier about it. I called her literally the night before. I got this brain storm. I said, 'You've got to come to work tomorrow in this movie.' There was no talk about reading the script or what the part was at all. She said, 'What should I look like?' I said, 'You should be *dark*'" – which gave Marlene the idea of putting together a costume of exotic odds and ends she had worn in previous pictures.[1]

Dietrich had been a collaborator and comrade of old – in 1943 she had replaced Rita Hayworth in *The Mercury Wonder Show* as the woman Welles sawed in half – but when he asked her to join him in the new film, it wasn't for a gathering of old cronies à la John Ford or Howard Hawks – he had had a glimpse of the part Dietrich would play in the film, if only that he had seen her as "*dark.*" German musician Paul Hindemith was once asked whether he had a clear idea of one of his compositions before he began to compose it, and he said that, yes, he did have an idea, but it was like seeing a landscape lit up by lightning – a vivid sense impression that he couldn't specify in the slightest detail, but would recognize when he saw it again, as he did when he began to compose it. Welles can't have known in detail how he was going to use Dietrich in *Touch of Evil,* and in fact it was the two of them working together during the shooting who actually developed her character and her lines. But it fits one's sense of how art works and how Welles worked to believe that he had seen that flash of lightning, and beneath the flash, a configuration of two characters

– Quinlan, the crooked cop he plays, and Dietrich's character, Tanya, a woman who runs a saloon, probably a whorehouse, in a Mexican town. When he and Dietrich came to filling in the details, they worked these characters and their relationship into the great thing in the film.

Touch of Evil is a well-made thriller about the machinations of a dishonest cop on the Mexican border. Welles directed it with the visual inventiveness and the instinct for unity of the master filmmaker he had become. There are brilliant virtuosic displays of the director's art – the celebrated one-take opening boom shot of everything going on in a border square – but Welles also lit his rich, dark sets with subtle harmony, so that the corrupt atmosphere of the film stays in the mind as a deep, alive, and unified visual experience and atmosphere. Apart from the handsome look of it, though, and the sense of high virtuosity at work, the thriller material in itself isn't very interesting, and much of it is thin, banal, even cheap. But the relation between Quinlan and Tanya is deeply interesting and substantial; although it is dramatized in only four scenes, it virtually holds the film together and is for many in the audience the main source of its value. Not only is it Tanya who voices the celebrated epitaph and elegy – and eulogy – for Quinlan at the end; she is the character from whose attitude toward him in her four brief appearances we have taken our cue about how to take Quinlan's whole character.

Captain Hank Quinlan is a great detective but a crooked cop in a town on the Mexican border; he plants evidence, frames suspects, blackmails, and even kills, for many conceivable reasons – to assert power or to demonstrate his infallible intuition about who is guilty of the crimes he is investigating, whatever the evidence – perhaps simply because being a crooked cop is his habitual behavior or his nature. The film follows his devious investigation of the car-bomb murder of a rich contractor named Linnekar. In the investigation, Quinlan puts up most unwillingly with the presence and the attempt at cooperation of a narcotics inspector from Mexico, named Vargas (Charlton Heston), who was on the scene when the murder took place and who involves himself in the investigation because the car and bomb came from across the border. Vargas's new American wife, Susie (Janet Leigh), is accompanying him; both become the butts of Quinlan's nasty anti-Mexican racism. At the climax of Quinlan's crooked investigation, his adoring partner, Menzies (Joseph Calleia), whose life Quinlan had saved years earlier, discovers the truth about his idol (Quinlan has given himself away by leaving his cane on the scene after murdering a minor mobster named Uncle Joe Grandi), and Menzies cooperates with Vargas to get down on tape the proof that Quinlan has framed the suspect in the Linnekar murder (who happens, ironically, to be guilty after all – Quinlan's intuition wins again). In the denouement, Quinlan shoots Menzies – with Vargas's gun, in order to implicate the Mexican – and then tries to shoot Vargas, but is himself shot by Menzies just before Menzies dies.

Quinlan is shapelessly fat and repulsively ugly, padded out to be even fatter than Welles himself was at the time; his doughy, pudgy, often sweaty face has few individualizing lines of character or expression, except for the unappetizing life in his fat-embedded eyes. The crafty and perverse intelligence in those eyes is always mean-spirited and sour. We get to know this man and his behavior extremely well, because Welles's camera and scenario bring him uncomfortably, disgustingly close to us, and Welles the actor is just as unsparing.

It is only after we have seen perhaps more than enough of this repellent man that we meet Tanya, an improbably gaudy inhabitant of the underworld who, we are surprised to learn, has a connection with Quinlan. There is an immense physical contrast between them, though, and it's amazing that there should be any connection between people who come from such different orders of humanity. Their relation isn't dramatic; they aren't engaged in an action with each other; it is the mere fact that these people know each other that matters. Unlike us, she isn't disgusted by him – she takes him as he comes, and this attitude brings an entirely unexpected moral depth and imagination to the film. Her way of reacting to Quinlan's terrible character and behavior steadies and clarifies our thinking; she accepts him with the gravity and equanimity that characterize everything about her. And it is the ease with which Dietrich's performance embodies those moral qualities of Tanya that makes her judgment matter.

That Tanya runs a bordello is something we gather from her costume and style rather than from anything we see happening. What we actually see her doing are routine tasks – cleaning up after closing her place, straightening out her accounts. The way she moves, even the way she sits, seems oddly competent, however firmly her makeup and costume place her in the world of gambling and sex. Her far-out makeup is artificial to the point of caricature – she is a virtual cartoon. Her made-up face is at once impassive and intensely expressive – it's a mask, full of meaning, but beyond individuality and almost beyond humanity; it doesn't register her thoughts or feelings of the moment. Her great unwavering eyes see everything and know everything. Though she seems to have no project in life beyond day-by-day existence, she seems guided by some strong commitment. All in all, especially in contrast with Quinlan, there is a harmony

"The unappetizing life in his fat-embedded eyes": Welles as Hank Quinlan. (Photo courtesy of Photofest)

about her, a coherence, almost a clarity of spirit, and it is partly this that gives her the authority to pass judgment on Quinlan – only her clear eyes can see him without bias. Quinlan's slovenly, pasty disorder stands pictorially at the opposite pole to Tanya's coherence and order. She ought to despise him as much as we do. If she is exempt from our repulsion about Quinlan, it is not through understanding all and forgiving all; that formula isn't her style. She accepts him with the equanimity of her entire approach to experience.

Quinlan is the central character, the film is about him, he is the character we follow – Welles is said to have rewritten the script to give prominence to the character he was going to play. And despite his repulsiveness and our reluctance to deal with him, we can't help paying him fascinated attention. Vargas too is involved in the action most of the time, but for all his busy activity, we invest no curiosity or interest in him, whereas after our first encounter with Quinlan we are under a constant pressure to figure him out. *Touch of Evil* wouldn't be important – not even for the tour de force of its famous opening sequence – if Quinlan weren't so fascinating, so problematic and so awful, and if Tanya didn't treat him so interestingly. She doesn't treat him with warmth or sympathy – the bond between them doesn't work with that kind of feeling; nor does the remarkable bond between Quinlan and the audience that gradually forms.

Tanya doesn't seem concerned with the reasons behind Quinlan's behavior, and we take this as advice to us not to be concerned either. Late in the film, when he is seriously drunk, he says that his wife was strangled to death many years before, that the guilty "half-breed" escaped, and that he has done nothing since but think about this terrible event – and drink, until he went on the wagon twelve years before. (It is when he is beginning to conspire with Uncle Joe Grandi to implicate Susie Vargas in a drug setup that he starts to drink again.) Later, when his confession is being drawn out by Menzies, to be put on tape, Menzies asks him whether he thought of his wife when he was strangling Grandi, and he answers that he thinks of nothing else, "except my job, my dirty job." All this has its effect, but his motives don't really matter to us very much or very long, for we are following Tanya's incurious lead. He hints that at some time in the past he had an affair with her, and we don't disbelieve this, but when she actually appears in the film she certainly isn't propelled by this motive but by chance, just as Dietrich had appeared by chance to Welles in the making of the film. While Quinlan is walking through the streets of the Mexican town across the border, he hears the sound of the pianola in Tanya's saloon and is drawn to it. He used to frequent the saloon but hasn't been there for a long time; she turns him away because she doesn't recognize him. When he tells her who he is, her reaction is first a quickly concealed amazement at the change in him, but what follows is neither welcoming nor unwelcoming – this is the initiation of the equanimity of her acceptance. But she does make him an occasion for her wit.

Tanya wields her wit with the pride and self-delight of a professional entertainer, all self-presentation, all style. The first thing she says, "We're closed," means only that the saloon is closed for the night and that Quinlan has changed so much that she doesn't recognize him as one of the people who might be admitted after hours; but Dietrich, by intonation and especially by provocatively hesitant timing, colors this statement of

Two great self-performers: Dietrich as Tanya is the other one. (Photo courtesy of Photofest)

fact with freewheeling innuendo, suggestive of nothing in particular, but setting the stage for richly complex tones to come. Her wit licenses her toughness. She explains why she failed to recognize Quinlan by a wisecrack, "You should lay off those candy bars"; by now her tone is comradely and good-humored. Quinlan's face meanwhile is registering a nearly imbecilic erotic pleasure at being in her presence: "I sure wish it was your chili I was getting fat on. Anyway, you're sure looking good." The devastating answer would be brutal if it didn't come in the format of a stand-up comedian. "You're a mess, honey." He continues his fatuous courtship: "That pianola sure brings back memories," an invitation that she wearily turns down and turns into a marketing discussion: "The customers go for it – it's so old, it's new. We've got the television too. We run movies. What can I offer you?" She has perfect freedom of tone with Quinlan, utterly untouched by the tension he usually generates around himself; her authority is far greater than his.

In Dietrich's performance the Wellesian theatrical art of self-impersonation is at its richest and deepest, wittiest, most completely together. Just as we always realized we were seeing the self-performing young Orson Welles when we saw the young Kane, now when we see Tanya, we are just as aware that we are seeing another great self-performer, Marlene Dietrich. Despite the discrepancy between Dietrich and her surroundings, this is indeed the famous star. Or is it? Her face and voice are so stylized, so emphatically Dietrich's, that she – or somebody else – might almost be giving an impersonation of Dietrich. But we naturally enough take her identity in good faith, as we do her theatrical impersonation of a character called Tanya. If we never forget that we are seeing Dietrich, that makes her Tanya even more artful, layered, and self-conscious than it would otherwise be.

By enlisting Dietrich, Welles brought into the film a rich array of implications. Her glamorous international stardom is at work here and certainly at play. It remained constant throughout her career, following her through her celebrated ups and downs, declines and comebacks. She remained a star even when for a time she was embarrassingly too visible a has-been – a great star who wasn't getting any roles. Theatrical impersonation of sexual authority remained her steady routine, too, guaranteed by well-publicized offscreen love affairs. And she had another idiomatic star quality, which is at the heart of her role in *Touch of Evil* – she was always the most highly organized person around, in her life as well as in her art.

Tanya's celebrated epitaph/elegy/eulogy for Quinlan at the end, the full articulation of her view of him, is couched in high rhetoric and covers a wide range of attitudes. Staring into the foul water into which Quinlan has fallen, she asks Schwartz, the assistant district attorney, "Isn't somebody going to come and take him away?" – she seems to want to shield from others Quinlan's bare animal identity; yet one hears a note of shame. She participates in the feelings about his death but only up to a point. When Schwartz calls Quinlan "a great detective, all right," she adds, "And a lousy cop" – her judgment of Quinlan remains clearheaded. When Schwartz asks, "You really liked him, didn't you?" she avoids her own feelings to answer, perhaps with greater intimacy and certainly with greater understanding of the situation, "The cop did, the one who killed him. He loved him." Asked again about her own feelings, she answers, in celebrated words, "He was some kind of a man," and closes the subject with, "What does it matter what you say about people?" We can hear Hamlet's eulogy of his father – "He was a man. Take him for all in all, / I shall not look upon his like again" – sounding behind all these words, with confused and even somewhat fraudulent implications of rich thinking and feeling. The words skillfully avoid conventional moral categories, really all categories, and yet Tanya's obliquity – "some kind of a man" – is perhaps more accurately read as a realistic glance at Quinlan's untrustworthiness and dishonesty, rather than as the overstuffed, slightly factitious, fluently generalizing rhetoric of understatement usually found in it. She puts a name to his crimes – "a lousy cop" – yet the whole passage resounds with, "Judge not, that ye be not judged." "What does it matter what you say about people?" carries acceptance into nihilism: 'What difference does anything make?' Nihilism suits Tanya's wit, her style, her uninflected speech, her self-sufficiency. But her denial of value seems to be protecting Quinlan from a wrong kind of judgment. Her valediction eludes ordinary moral naming – the tonelessness of "say about people" sounds fed up with making judgments – and yet despite all the evasion, this elegy remarkably turns out in the end to be a eulogy, too, conveying an unmistakable sense of Quinlan's importance.

Tanya's attitude toward Quinlan is corroborated by the different levels of illusion combining at this moment: Tanya herself, Dietrich (always audible), Welles's uniquely rounded performance and the screenplay written to accommodate it, and the whole overall intention of *Touch of Evil*. We hear the intention of the actors and writer and director clearly behind this moment of highly contrived eloquence, and instead of spoiling the illusion, the doubling deepens the expression in this theatrical art. Just as the audience's thrilled consciousness of being in the presence of Dickens at one of his readings didn't interfere with their experiencing the illusion of the murder of Nancy in *Oliver Twist* but rather added an alluring intensity to that illusion, so the fact that we are encountering Marlene Dietrich, oddly appearing in a role too small for her and in a film that isn't really her sort, doesn't destroy the illusion that we are seeing Tanya, the madame of a whorehouse in a Mexican town, who also happens to be, like Dietrich, something of an authority about human weakness – and the circle goes around again. It isn't only Tanya's judgment of Quinlan that we hear in the end, but also Dietrich's, and Welles's, and the film's, as is borne out by the quality of the language, which is heavy not only with meaning but with style. Tanya's sentences are rightly famous, but none of them is exactly "in character" in the ordinary sense of the phrase. Neither Tanya, Dietrich, nor Welles himself has suddenly been transfigured into a paragon of stylish expression; the often parodied lines are if anything riper and gamier in the theatrical rhetoric of high camp than the rest of Tanya's language. These words come perhaps too close to camp to be weighed so solemnly, and some who accept them most eagerly as valuable may be tone-deaf to the issues of sincerity of expression they cunningly raise. But experienced admirers of *Touch of Evil* will all along have been agreeably aware of the rich mixture of modes they have been dealing with, and as instances of performance art in the movies, Tanya's lines are unrivaled.

Dietrich's final scene is her own achievement, but also the beneficiary of Welles's supreme ease with the medium, which lets him avail himself fluently of all of cinema's resources of eloquence. The separable elements of the complex effect are of the highest quality: Dietrich's face, always intrinsically expressive, meaningful even when uninflected; her equal skill and wit in intonation and projection; and the long practice at presenting herself and her image by which she and the cinematographer have learned how to capture both her aura and her essence. The densely velvety, sumptuous light provided for her by the lighting engineer intensifies the glow of her image; and the expertise of the sound engineers reduces her perfectly spoken lines to a marvelously unemphatic quietness with no clutter of superfluous resonance. The star is being given star treatment; the ceremony of glamour is being celebrated, to glorify the star and to honor the medium of film – and partly, to be sure, to enhance the prestige of Welles. But the ceremony is *working*, in the service of intensest expressivity and the complex meaning, working with precision and with passion – and it is also working with the perfectly audible ambition of creating a great moment of theatrical art.

Our sense of Quinlan's depth here isn't of course solely the work of Tanya/Dietrich's understanding of him or of the collaboration between Dietrich and Welles. Quinlan is one of Welles's masterworks. He wrote the role for himself and presented himself with such rich candor that he made it easily his greatest role. He had never made himself so repellent before, and that opportunity may have been the fascination of the role and of the whole film for him. Many details show how much he relished playing Quinlan. For this repellent toad he wittily fashioned a brilliantly theatrical entrance; Quinlan's arrival is prepared for by the falsest of expectations in a time-tested strategy of narrative, his approach heralded by effusive praise not only from the slavish Menzies but also from District Attorney Adair (Ray Collins) and his staff. All is expectant apprehension and anxiety; nothing must be touched until the arrival of the great detective, who will instantly straighten everything out, and so forth. The images of competence and authority so aroused are wittily exploded by our first glimpse of Quinlan, stuffed into the front seat of his car, hardly able to get himself out except, it seems, by appealing to the force of gravity for release. But if the predicament of this bloated figure is for a moment straightforwardly funny as well as wittily repulsive, that is the only joke in the characterization.

Once Quinlan has arrived and is at work, the other characters do indeed, as predicted, respect him, defer to him, fear him. There are hints that he has more than merely natural powers – his figure and behavior seem to have a near-totemic virtue for his colleagues. But the Quinlan Welles is interested in is not a figure of grand charisma. His speciality is in sly and self-tickled nuances of meanness and nastiness – the performance is richly detailed in squalid malice. It's also impressively coherent – a strong continuity binds these details together; it's always the same person we're watching. We know Quinlan is always tasting the same corrosive bitterness in his mouth, even at a hideous moment when he listens with exaggerated, sheepish humility to Menzies's fawning praise. When Quinlan smiles in this awful scene, his face crumples up to a shapelessness of delight close to ecstasy, and we seem to look deeply and with disgust into the syrup of his self-loving falsity.

After his theatrical entrance, he mutes his grotesqueness and moves his misshapen body with surprising energy and competence as he goes about his job. The different aspects of his behavior fold into each other smoothly to create a single character: now persistent, now mean, now sneering, now impetuous, now unexpectedly tactful and kind when he sympathizes with Linnekar's daughter (getting no response from that cold young woman), often sour, always competent. His naughtiest racist insults often have an ulterior motive. When he tells Menzies at the top of his voice to accompany Vargas into the other room because Vargas may not know how to use an American phone, he is enjoying his own racism but also protecting the frame-up he is engineering.

One witty surprise in his self-dramatization goes outside the character to merge with Welles's own self-dramatization. When Quinlan throws his badge down on the table in righteous indignation at being accused by Vargas of tampering with evidence, Welles springs a self-referential joke. As Quinlan is leaving the room, very dramatically, moving toward the back of the set, he is heard to say, "I won't take back that badge until the people of this county vote it back" – and the last words trail off in the exact accents of Charles Foster Kane's most pompous words about his relation with "the people." Welles asks an enormous range of expression of himself in this film – at the end, when he leers grotesquely but also eerily, like a madman, as he is about to shoot Vargas, his face is a cartoon of rage, almost doll-like, the eyes little agitated buttons of malevolence; just before his death his face and whole body, in a triumph of makeup and impersonation, melt into a greasy, sweat-and-fat-filled bag of animal hopelessness and despair.

Quinlan's doughy face is nevertheless the most alive in the film, always giving a comprehensive and vivid report of the mind behind it. He is the most expressive character in the film – excepting always and only, at the other end of the spectrum, the paradoxically high expressivity of Tanya's impassive mask. Quinlan's nerve-wracking and malevolent vitality lacks the glamour and dignity of the demonic; the evil we read in his face is more ordinary – sly nasty teasing, mischief, cheap pleasure in his own misbehavior. He can hardly believe his luck at meeting Vargas, a Mexican government official, married to a blonde American woman. He loves it, and he isn't joking or teasing – the hope of reviling and humiliating is clear.

Since Welles is playing the role, Quinlan is gifted with Welles's splendidly resonant voice, perhaps disconcertingly at first, but we are soon able to attribute it to the power of the character. The voice is less mellifluous, rougher and more abrasive than usual, but it retains the command and timbre of authority Welles's voice always had, and if Quinlan's power is perversely attractive as well as repellent, Welles's seductive voice has a lot to do with it.

In Quinlan's second encounter with Tanya, his despair is open and intense, and it doesn't in the least ennoble him. The scene comes toward the end of the film, toward the end of his life, and clearly marks his fear of death. He has just strangled Uncle Joe Grandi, having framed Susie Vargas for the crime to get Vargas out of the way; he has come to Tanya's saloon to drink, perhaps in some nameless horror at what he has done, and is now in a state of filthy, final drunkenness, barely able to move. When he collects himself, he bursts in on her importunately to get her to tell him his fortune. When she is reluctant, he pulls out the cards himself and spreads them angrily over the table on which she is doing her accounts: "Tell me my future," he demands, and she looks up at him with impassivity as she answers, with the brevity of an oracle, "You haven't got any," and then in another Delphic utterance, "Your future's all used up." Quinlan has been having a premonition, and her reluctance, which at first seemed just refusal to be bothered, now suggests that she doesn't need the cards to see that Quinlan is finished. Tanya's colloquial language makes this moment poignant as well as electrifying. Taken as a statement, "Your future's all used up," merely repeats the point already made, but "all used up" softens the message and almost makes it tender – as if she were explaining something to a child. From then on we take Quinlan as the doomed man she has told him he is, and we listen to him in the light of this oracle. Yet even Tanya's omniscience hasn't prepared us – or even, apparently, herself – for the degradation of his end – the betrayal by his loving disciple Menzies, justified and agonizedly reluctant but still betrayal, with all that implies for Quinlan's pleasure in his power over men; the ignoble loss of balance and backward fall into the filthy sumplike water – afterward we can tell only by dim glimpses in the dark and at a distance what has happened to the unloved and unlovely body.

Besides the characters of Quinlan and Tanya and the relation between them, there is one other important strength in *Touch of Evil,* which the seldom trustworthy David Thomson caught exactly in his biography of Welles, *Rosebud:* "*Touch of Evil* is a continuous and consistent stylistic reverie on claustrophobia and corruption."[2] "Reverie" sounds an irrelevantly lyric note, but "continuous and consistent" are exactly right: *Touch of Evil* is indeed fully and richly charged throughout with the atmosphere of corruption Thomson is speaking about; it's a look and a meaning, a smell, that binds everything together and remains in the mind afterward. Welles is entirely in charge here, controlling and unifying his materials, unfolding the action with great speed, variety, and fluidity, inserting shots of dark squares and streets into the action with tactful irregularity, controlling our visual experience of the film by subtle gradations of black-and-white tones, and by the sheen of the black light of night. The steady propulsive excitement of the editing plays a major part in the overall effect.

Dark corruption is suggested immediately in the one-take opening scene, the most famous piece of virtuosity in Welles's career. We are looking down from a high angle onto a busy Mexican square, at night, and while we look through the camera's eye in the slow sweeping movement of the boom shot that covers the whole area of the square, we see an action, the key action of the film, the entire progress of a murder, from the moment when a bomb is attached to a car, through the car's maneuvering in the complicated traffic of the square, past the customs control at the border, and then on to the explosion. The camera is also watching the progress of Vargas and Susie, as they make their way across the square to the border control; they connect for a moment or two with the car that is about to be destroyed, and they are kissing when the bomb explodes. The interest and power of the scene come from the sense of mastery with which we watch the whole of it; but our sense of mastery is a kind of illusion, for we watch with only half-comprehension, not knowing which, if any, of these people are doomed. Meanwhile, the scene solidly inaugurates not only the atmosphere of the film that follows but its main action.

It is puzzling why the continuous atmosphere of corruption doesn't or cannot collect the weaker elements in the film into itself and give more life to them, or at least frame them more effectively, for though the minor characters are much involved in the corruption, they gain minimal interest from that involvement. Vargas and his new bride, Susie, are directly threatened by the corrupt atmosphere and doings of the town; the chief instruments of that threat are Uncle Joe Grandi, his hotel, the Grandi boys, and their motel. But apart from Akim Tamiroff as Uncle Joe Grandi, all this material is weak and empty, much of it is cheap, and the level of cliché is high.

The relation between the newlywed Vargas and Susie is a clumsy and callow, empty pattern of separations and reunions, without rhythm. It would be a pleasure to take it ironically, but there's no guidance from the film to do so. Welles seems to have thought he could animate Susie's character by having her handle Grandi and his gang with chirpy spunkiness instead of anxiety, but it isn't much of an idea, and Leigh can't bring off so tricky an assignment, though a familiar American nastiness was her specialty; she lacks charm and presence throughout, as does Charlton Heston as Vargas. Welles himself is responsible for the casting of Leigh, but he didn't cast Heston, who, indeed, virtually cast Welles. While Heston was considering whether to accept his part in the proposed film, the studio as an inducement told him, "We have Welles," meaning that Welles was signed on to play Quinlan; Heston thought it meant that Welles was going to direct, and got so excited at the prospect of working with the great man that producer Albert Zugsmith did offer the assignment to Welles. Welles on many occasions expressed his gratitude and appreciation for Heston's generosity, rightly, and he seems never to have been troubled by Heston's inadequacy; perhaps he told himself that he would surely be able to summon or create something new and alive in an actor who had the good taste to admire Orson Welles so much. But Heston in the guise of a Mexican narcotics officer in *Touch of Evil* is the same stiff straight-arrow earnest civics teacher he impersonated throughout his career. Neither Leigh nor Heston had star power, but they unfortunately seem to have had the yearnings toward it, and perhaps it was that goal that inhibited them from learning the unemphatic naturalness that helped to make many less well-known principal players in Hollywood films useful, and helped them swell that vivid profusion of life that is one of the facts about the art of Hollywood. Naturalness would actually have been more readily learned from the stars, but it would have taken more intelligent actors than Heston and Leigh to grasp that.

Welles may in any case not have been particularly good at directing ordinarily good-looking leading actors. Rita Hayworth is completely effective in *The Lady from Shanghai,* and must to some extent have been well directed, but this surely is a special case, since she must have felt a dramatically useful special bond with Welles, despite the impending divorce. Though Welles's strained relations with her must have had something to do with the blank lack of erotic tension between the lovers, in particular with his wooden behavior as a lover, some part of this may be ascribed to a general limitation in Welles's skills as a director of non-character roles – he couldn't even direct himself in this kind of role. The young Anne Baxter, just emerging as a star, is beautiful and skillful in *The Magnificent Ambersons,* easily projecting the charm, wit, and grace her role requires. But she projects an interesting intelligence, too, and her success may be due to intelligent self-direction. Joseph Cotten, in his early days a normally handsome leading man, had become a gifted and experienced major actor, as he is in *Ambersons*; he was Welles's equal in experience, and there was a long personal association between them; it's likely that he too directed himself. Apart from these few, Welles's successful characters are all vivid and far-out eccentrics – fitting easily into Welles's theatrical method.

When Welles changed the Heston character to a Mexican in rewriting the screenplay, he must have been intending to up the ethnic mix to feed Quinlan's bias; but perhaps he was also trying to counteract Heston's Arrow-shirt-ad looks and style. However, it's not clear whether he was as troubled by Heston's style as we are. He had shortly before chosen the even more wooden Robert Arden as the straight lead in *Mr. Arkadin,* an actor who contributed even less competence and no box-office appeal. Welles could do nothing with Arden, though he must have believed he could, and he probably believed he actually did; and perhaps the same is true of Heston, who was not his choice.

In truth all these not-very-gifted straight actors weren't given much to work with. Welles's screenplay created for Dietrich and himself two richly and powerfully written characterizations – given some lines that are marvels of invention – but it offered the lesser players hardly anything. It is poignant to see how winnowed of strength Ray Collins had become as he aged; yet his skill and know-how can still make the points of an alive characterization – but how little he got to do as the district attorney! Joseph Calleia as Menzies is altogether moving and admirable, yet the spaniel aspect of the role is so excruciatingly convincing that it's sometimes hard to take. What the other characters were asked to do was often oddly wrong. Whether or not we're meant to think the young newlyweds' canoodling in their convertible tiresome isn't clear, and the cute antagonism between them is painfully off-key and over a long stretch of the action; it's pointlessly implausible that Vargas should leave his new wife at a motel that anyone can spot as the locus classicus of sinister danger. Susie's reaction to the loud music the Grandi boys are using to make her hysterical is a thin and tinny sketch of fear, photographed too often in exactly the same terms, as is the threatening approach of the banal Grandi boys and their molls, the repeated suspense shots of the slowly turning doorknob, and the rest of the stale vocabulary of menace which for some reason attracted the interest of Welles; the lifelessness of the editing of the whole sequence suggests that Welles had virtually given up the game. Since it's so clearly the need of the plot that created the Grandi boys and their molls, just to scare us – and no emotional need generated inside the action – we know that nothing serious and final is going to happen, and nothing does happen; and for people like myself who overrespond to the suspenseful threat of violence even when we know none is coming, the fakery of this whole episode leaves us feeling squalidly exploited. Not that some vile action is required; as with any failure, one doesn't know in advance what success would have looked like. Yet recharging the theme of corruption and evil was the task of the action in the motel, and it didn't happen.

It seems clear that Welles was simply uninterested. The whole machinery of Grandi evil is thinly realized – too many sinister smiles of Latino hoods and drifters and hopheads, seen too often as they menacingly cross too many dark streets. Lack of inventiveness is almost thrust on our attention and judgment. One of the members of the Grandi gang is initially a convincing enough hophead, bobbing and twitching promisingly; the viewer would accept more, and he does in fact reappear, but inexplicably quieted down – there is nothing for him to do, and he plays no role in the action of group menace. Did something go wrong? Something more than what the film shows must have been planned for Mercedes McCambridge as a gang member. The disappearance of this powerful actress into ineffectuality inside the film, and then her literal disappearance from the film, seem emblematic. This whole motel nightmare is a half-hearted charade of cut-rate horror effects, rather than something deeply imagined. Welles was enthusiastic about Dennis Weaver, who plays the slightly crazy clerk at the motel, and others have been impressed by the pathological sexual curiosity they find in this character; but whatever effect Weaver makes at the beginning is counteracted by the repetitiveness of his behavior.

Against this continuing impression that Welles is spinning his wheels in these scary scenes at the middle of the film, Quinlan's murder of Grandi stands out as a real action, to say the least. As we begin to watch with undisguised anticipated pleasure Tamiroff's performance in this scene, we feel happy to be given over again into such greatly gifted hands, and such an experienced and witty intelligence – he is a strong asset in the film's accounting, providing much incidental pleasure. But by the time of the murder, Grandi's corruption has worn thin through overexposure and so, to an unfortunate extent, has our amusement at Tamiroff's antics, taken merely as theatrical routines. The murder seems motiveless on Quinlan's part – Grandi is being gratuitously but also quite implausibly sacrificed as part of the scheme to frame Susie – and therefore the cliché elements of the scene (alternating light and darkness from a sign outside the hotel window, Tamiroff's fearful grimaces, the implacably tightening garrote, the whole machinery of horror) seem applied externally just to scare us, just by the will of the director, who we discover later on was all the while doing some slow cooking on the one effect he must have really liked: an upside-down shot of the head of the dead Tamiroff, eyes bulging, hanging over the headboard of Susie's bed – an apparition meant to scare Janet Leigh and all of us almost to death.

The film's dark atmosphere of corruption regains its power and its sense of motive in the last sequence, in which Vargas trails Quinlan and Menzies with his tape recorder, under bridges, beside embankments, over and under all kinds of debris; its use of space and lighting is reminiscent of the opening sequence. The sequence is beautiful to look at in itself, for the gleams of reflected light in the blackness and for its variegated details of urban squalor, oil wells, marine paraphernalia; the action is mapped out with beautiful legibility, Vargas's white shirt serving as the guide. By the end every inch of the screen seems to have been covered, and the blackness seems to have collected all earlier blackness into itself – it is a deservedly expansive coda to the film. The action is firmly moved ahead by simple suspense about when Quinlan will discover that his confession of having murdered Grandi is being recorded; that discovery satisfyingly produces the rapid commotion and gunplay that lead to the final actions – the death of Menzies and eventually of Quinlan. The movement of the night scene comes to climax and emotional resolution, ironically, in the confused and humiliated movements of Quinlan near death – at bay, trying one last time to bluff Vargas, shot by Menzies, falling into the water. And then, the blackness setting off her unrivaled and luminous face, Tanya comes to speak the elegy that gathers Quinlan's life into her acceptance.

6

Welles's Shakespeare

Welles's Shakespeare films were made with inadequate budgets, which he never figured out how to circumvent or disguise. The lack of money made a difference, of course, but less than one might expect, though it makes judgment of these films tricky. You can see the scantness of Welles's resources plainly in the pitifully meager sets and costumes of *Macbeth*; you can hear it in the echoing, out-of-sync soundtrack of parts of *Chimes at Midnight;* much of *Othello* is badly dubbed, and there are other, less noticeable flaws in all the films. One understands and sympathizes, of course; but the consequences don't disappear for all that, but remain stubbornly and distractingly right in the middle of one's experience of the films.

So does something more important for which Welles was more responsible – the way he cut the texts. Nobody really cares how or how much he changed the pop novels on which he based *The Lady from Shanghai* or *Touch of Evil,* which in fact realized their ideal destiny in Welles's transformations. *Citizen Kane* was based on an original screenplay by Welles and Mankiewicz, and therefore raised no issue about fidelity to sources. But *The Magnificent Ambersons* did raise the issue, ironically and in the end painfully. The whole equivocal process has been dealt with in Chapter 3; it is a sad story, which doesn't in the least redound to Welles's discredit.

Welles's faithfulness to the Shakespeare texts he filmed is more complicated and more problematic, and these texts have such prestige and are so alive in so many minds that serious questions about these revisions inevitably arise. Many of the revisions are troubling. The defects of Welles's Shakespeare cuts can so occupy one's attention that they threaten to spoil the whole experience. Yet sometimes, somehow, in an odd, almost magical process, this doesn't happen. Problems in a Welles Shakespeare film can simply drop away from consciousness, leaving behind only a sense of Welles's fresh and direct feeling for the plays. With *Macbeth,* one can seem stuck forever in the world of those awful walls of mud pretending to be stone, a world of dowdy, characterless costumes, which form shapeless and unsuggestive images on the screen; but then, suddenly, the inadequacy of walls and costumes, the vague images, become eloquent, suggesting the dark nothingness of death or the squalor of killing, the very "fog and filthy air" the witches invoke. Welles's special feeling for this play is making itself known, as is the power of his natural instinct for making expressive art.

Macbeth

When Welles came to preparing a text for *Macbeth,* he was on familiar ground – he was a Shakespeare lover of the old school. His connection with Shakespeare developed early, went deep, and remained central to his life as an artist. He got it partly from the culture in which he grew up (the range and depth of the musical and theatrical life in the Midwest of the early twentieth century, which ought to make Eastern snobbishness ashamed of itself) and partly from Roger Hill, his great teacher and headmaster at the Todd School. It was no merely pious reverence for the Bard that teacher and student shared but sophisticated understanding and respect, together with the knowledgeability of practical professionals. While studying Shakespeare as a schoolboy at Todd with Hill, Welles produced his first stagings of the plays (including his first attempt at what became *Chimes at Midnight* more than three decades later) with the school's excellent theatrical facilities; they sound remarkable in the depth of their understanding. Soon afterward he collaborated with Hill, apparently on equal terms, in preparing school editions of *Twelfth Night, The Merchant of Venice,* and *Julius Caesar.* He knew great sections of Shakespeare by heart and often used Shakespeare's language to guide his seeing and feeling in daily life. And though his films of *Macbeth* and *Othello* and *Chimes at Midnight* were made under differing conditions and are all flawed in some degree, they are all visibly alive with the passion and pleasure that must have been rooted in his early days – they are full of the infectious sound of someone fully engaged on the most important project imaginable.

When in 1936, at the age of twenty-one, he directed *Macbeth* for the Federal Theatre in New York and shortly thereafter *Julius Caesar* for his own Mercury Theatre, he rather surprisingly chose a style that would today be called *high concept.* He reshaped the texts aggressively, shifting the action into time and locales quite different from Shakespeare's, seriously changing the tone and meaning of the original. In *Macbeth* he changed medieval Scotland into nineteenth-century Haiti, and Shakespeare's remote, ambiguous witches into seductively throbbing images drawn from vital voodoo ritual and religion, and in *Julius Caesar* he transformed ancient Rome under the Caesars into Rome as a modern fascist state. These revisions played a big part in Welles's early fame, for though high-concept theater was not unknown in 1936, it hadn't before been offered with such panache in America.

This style has unfortunately become preeminent today, the common practice of our directors of Shakespeare and other classic dramatists; it is seen everywhere in England, and in the state-supported theaters of Germany, and elsewhere in continental Europe it so prevails that it seems almost to be mandated by law – likewise with its counterpart in opera production. Its attraction is no great mystery, since it frees directors from obedience to circumstances dictated by playwrights, who are regarded in this philosophy as oppressive, hegemonic tyrants – high concept licenses these directors to get into the act themselves, to rethink a play on their own by inventing quite different conditions in which its action might take place – with the avowed purpose, to be sure, of generating new insight into that action, however puzzling it is to discover what insight emerges from the kind of choices made in the name of this style. High concept has such control these days that traditional productions are automatically ticked off as signs of a director's incapacity as a creative artist. The 1984 production of Beckett's *Endgame* at the American Repertory Theater in Cambridge, Massachusetts, was an almost comically illustrative example. JoAnne Akalaitis, the director, recruited expressly for her knack of twisting familiar works into unrecognizable new forms, had her moment of Creative Vision about this play when she conceived the idea of placing the action of the play not in the room that Beckett meticulously described in his text (two small windows, high up, a door, a picture with its face to the wall, and so on) but in an abandoned subway car. Beckett heard about this and objected, taking the reasonable line that his stage directions were an integral part of the substance of the play he had given the ART permission to produce. There followed acrimonious debate about free speech, the creative imagination, the death of the author, the total authority of the director, and the irrevelance of common sense as a criterion of judgment in art; and then Beckett made what the Akalaitis supporters must have thought a really oppressive claim of hegemony over the play by refusing to allow Akalaitis's version to be presented over his name. The ART's ludicrous final position was to present *Endgame* as an anonymous work.

Welles's high-concept theater of 1936 was far less arbitrary and doctrinaire than this, lacking the systematic ideological imperatives of the Continental models of the fifties and sixties. It sounds as if it had been a young man's ingenuous natural fantasy that brought the ideas of Haiti and Italian fascism to Welles's mind, whereas in high concept the grinding wheels of the arbitrary are just what is wanted and in fact relished when locales are changed against all reason. In any case, Welles soon abandoned this style. When he staged *King Lear* and the Henry history plays several times during his career, and when he filmed *Macbeth* (1948), *Othello* (1952), and his own redaction of the Henry plays, *Chimes at Midnight* (1966), Welles used costumes and locales pretty much like those in traditional productions – if by necessity sadly cheaper, less splendid, and less solid – and he presented the plays themselves straightfowardly as Renaissance humanist dramas of individual character, desire, and will, as he had been taught them, instead of subverting or deconstructing these characteristics and meanings.

But this doesn't mean that he had turned into an original-instrument sort of purist when he dealt with Shakespeare's text. He remained a champion cutter and rearranger, sometimes capricious and often plain wrong. Some of his cutting is the kind Shakespeare stage directors do as a matter of course and almost have to do, granted the time constraints of modern theatical performance. Welles cut the curious scene (IV.iii) in which Malcolm confesses monstrous fictive sins to Macduff in order to test his character, and many stage directors have also cut this scene, which seems next to impossible to put over in the theater. Many directors regularly condense Shakespeare's long passages of exposition writing to get on with the action; so Welles was not out of line with general practice when he cut the whole second scene of *Macbeth,* which is all expository narrative, no "action." But this, unlike cutting the rather artificial Malcolm–Macduff scene, gives up too much.

In this scene (I.ii), a soldier makes a report to Duncan, praising Macbeth's feats in the battle just ended:

> For brave Macbeth (well he deserves that name),
> Disdaining Fortune, with his brandish'd steel,
> Which smok'd with bloody execution,
> (Like Valor's minion) carv'd out his passage
> Till he fac'd the slave;
> Which nev'r shook hands, nor bade farewell to him,

Till he unseam'd him from the nave to th' chops,
And fix'd his head upon our battlements.
(I.ii.16–23)[1]

The reason this scene, particularly the quoted speech, should be saved is not because it makes particular points about character or action, but because of the power of its imagery, even though it is hard to be certain just how these unnervingly savage images of blood lust actually function in the play. The voluptuous sensuality of "smok'd" and "carv'd" and "unseam'd" exerts a dangerous temptation, inviting us to take pleasure in the glamour of bloodshed and the thrill of mastery over helpless human bodies at our mercy. And the images are virtually free-floating; we might expect them eventually to be placed in some exact relation with Macbeth's murder of Duncan, but nothing of that sort develops. On the face of it, there ought to be a connection between Macbeth's words "carv'd" and "unseam'd" and the fact that he later actually does "carve" Duncan, and actually makes his "brandish'd steel" smoke "with bloody execution," but this is a connection the play doesn't really make. Even Ross's all but clairvoyant praise of Macbeth as "Nothing afeared of what thyself didst make,/Strange images of death" (I.iii.96–97) doesn't have the effect of foretelling Macbeth's murder of Duncan – one senses a connection, yes, but it's elusive.

We are dealing with a typically Shakespearean habit, method, and skill; these vivid images don't describe Macbeth's character in particular or his way of killing in particular, but instead are generalizing images describing how any great and victorious soldier would perform. The characters speak from and about a world of war in which such barbarism is simply what happens. Soon afterward, Shakespeare smoothly shifts the emphasis, without notification, having Duncan praise Macbeth in the language of a world far closer to ours: "O valiant cousin! Worthy gentleman!" (I.ii.24) – not quite appropriate words for describing a soldier who fixes his enemy's head on the battlements, yet we don't really pay attention to the difference. Shakespeare is deeply and unflaggingly interested in character, but his art is never more flexible and interesting than when it is dismissing our awareness of a character because it is useful to do so at that moment, bringing it back when that in turn is useful. Duncan here is not a man with a particular personality, but a role, the role of a king gratefully receiving a report about his noble subject Macbeth's successful conduct in an important battle; he is not one kind of king or another, and his attitude toward the bloody behavior being reported to him is not of one kind or another. Nor is there any clear connection between this Duncan and the character who will soon pay sublime tribute to the benign atmosphere of Macbeth's castle:

> This castle hath a pleasant seat, the air
> Nimbly and sweetly recommends itself
> Unto our gentle senses.
> (I.vi.1–3)

Nor is Macbeth, as a soldier, presented as particularly interested in blood and cruelty, however much he has to do with both blood and cruelty in the battle and in his castle. He behaves the way he must behave to have "valor" and to be called "brave" in this world.

Yet we can grant all this and still not be quite at ease with the unsettling imagery of blood and cruelty that the second scene has laid on us. For if the imagery isn't saying something exact about the bloody and inhuman character of the play's hero, it does place him in a setting that is full of excitement about cruelty and violence, and powerfully interested in thinking and feeling about killing and death. Though we don't attach these implications to Macbeth in particular, once they are uttered they hover over the action and over Macbeth, coloring the atmosphere of the play, focusing and intensifying its exploration of the cause and dynamics of evil, while at the same time infinitely complicating what might otherwise be helpfully clear categories of good and evil. The scene has great weight, and feels important; it is unmistakably Shakespearean, in its power, and in the way it resists any attempt to untangle and paraphrase the way it achieves its effects; its unparaphrasability doesn't seem a liability, but a necessary condition of its dense energy of thought and feeling. Finally, after all this praise, it will nevertheless be obvious how strongly this puzzling scene with its dense Shakespearean imagery will tempt a time-stressed director to cut it – as Welles has done.

In another highly visible cut, Welles pared away to almost nothing the Porter's comic monologue as he goes to answer the knocking at the door, deleting a passage almost as familiar to American students of Shakespeare as "To be or not to be." This scene – its existence, at any rate – is so famous, in fact, that the cut may be a negative critical judgment, or even a joke. And with good reason. We have all been told how funny the Porter is, but his jokes today are only theoretically funny, and we don't really understand them, either; it looks as though Welles felt the same. It's not quite certain, though, since he cast Gus Schilling in the role, a favorite member of his regular troupe whose work he clearly liked, and he may have

Dunsinane and the arrival of Duncan (Erskine Sanford, with the white beard). Welles's Macbeth at center foreground; Roddy MacDowall as Malcolm, in the fur vest at right. (Photo courtesy of Photofest)

planned initially to keep more of the speech for him. But in the end he had no greater loyalty to the speech than we do.

Welles's really serious cuts in *Macbeth* are less visible. It takes close familiarity with the text to realize that he has chopped Macbeth's soliloquies into pieces and then moved the pieces around to spots in the action where their meaning gets changed. The fact that we may not notice that this is happening could mean that these cuts don't matter very much, and that is both the case and not the case. It's complicated.

The opening action in *Macbeth,* leading up to the murder of Duncan (Erskine Sanford), is driven by a series of dialogues between Macbeth and Lady Macbeth (Jeanette Nolan), interspersed with a series of Macbeth's soliloquies; the dialogues and the soliloquies embody in differing modes of dramaturgy Macbeth's thinking and feeling about the murder, as he approaches and accomplishes it. Here Shakespeare is working at the top of his bent as a dramatic poet. One might go to just these scenes – the dialogues between Macbeth and Lady Macbeth, and Macbeth's soliloquies – to show Shakespeare's unmatched capacity to use language to manifest the inner life of his characters. Hamlet's "O, what a rogue and peasant slave am I" is a marvelous achievement that deserves its fame, and it's brilliantly calculated to make us believe we are making contact with Hamlet's mind; but compared with Macbeth's "If it were done when 'tis done," it is less powerfully three-dimensional in registering a mind in operation, and therefore in its conception of what a mind in operation sounds and feels like.

Shakespeare's supreme powers in *Macbeth* produce more than vivid, deep registration of strokes of behavior. This is the play that contains not only Macbeth's soliloquies but his hallucination about the dagger, for instance – nobody had ever thought of that before; not only Lady Macbeth's invocations to evil but her sleepwalking scene – imagine seeing that for the first time; along with such staggering simplicities as her question, "Yet who would have thought the old man to have had so much blood in him?" (V.i.39–40) or the startling earlier invention, "Had he not resembled / My father as he slept, I had done't" (II.ii.12–13).

All of the various actions and ruminations in this huge action of Duncan's murder occur in a certain order. As we experience Macbeth's experiences of hesitation, fear, doubt, consciousness of guilt, focusing, and refocusing of will, we notice and are affected by the order in which all this occurs. The soliloquies are connected with major moments of the action. Macbeth speaks "Is this a dagger which I see before me, /The handle toward my hand?" (II.i.33–34) on his way to perform the murder, indeed, just before he commits it; the approach to the act seems to conjure up the hallucination, which then becomes a kind of rehearsal. Lady Macbeth had earlier worked with remorseless energy and passion to strengthen his resolve, and Shakespeare's amazing invention of the hallucination gets part of its force from our remembering the state of mind to which Lady Macbeth's successful manipulations had brought Macbeth:

I am settled, and bend up
Each corporal agent to this terrible feat.
Away, and mock the time with fairest show:
False face must hide what the false heart doth know.
(I.vii.79–82)

The little rhyming tag of the cadence, which sounds like proverbial wisdom, hints at something slightly bogus in Macbeth's resolution. And then comes the dagger:

Is this a dagger which I see before me,
The handle toward my hand? Come, let me clutch thee:

I have thee not, and yet I see thee still.
Art thou not, fatal vision, sensible
To feeling as to sight? or art thou but
A dagger of the mind, a false creation,
Proceeding from the heat-oppressed brain?
I see thee yet, in form as palpable
As this which now I draw.
Thou marshal'st me the way that I was going,
And such an instrument I was to use.
Mine eyes are made the fools o' th' other senses,
Or else worth all the rest. I see thee still;
And on thy blade and dudgeon gouts of blood,
Which was not so before. There's no such thing:
It is the bloody business which informs
Thus to mine eyes. Now o'er the one half world
Nature seems dead, and wicked dreams abuse
The curtain'd sleep; witchcraft celebrates
Pale Hecat's off'rings; and wither'd Murther,
Alarum'd by his sentinel, the wolf,
Whose howl's his watch, thus with his stealthy pace,
With Tarquin's ravishing strides, towards his design
Moves like a ghost. Thou sure and firm-set earth,
Hear not my steps, which way they walk, for fear
The very stones prate of my whereabout,
And take the present horror from the time,
Which now suits with it. Whiles I threat, he lives:
Words to the heat of deeds too cold breath gives.
[*A bell rings*]
I go, and it is done; the bell invites me.
Hear it not, Duncan, for it is a knell,
That summons thee to heaven, or to hell.
(II.i.33–64)

That hallucination doesn't in the end shake his will to proceed with the murder, as it might have before. Instead, he comes to terms with it in surprising self-knowledge about what's happening: "There's no such thing:/ It is the bloody business which informs/Thus to mine eyes." He strengthens his will by taking the world into partnership for the act he is about to perform: "Now o'er the one half world/Nature seems dead, and wicked dreams abuse/The curtain'd sleep." His nerves hold steady even through another kind of hallucination, as he watches an avatar of himself approaching Duncan to kill him, his murderous motive thickly encrusted with evil analogs and portents: "and withered Murther, /Alarum'd by his sentinel, the wolf, /Whose howl's his watch, thus with his stealthy pace, / With Tarquin's ravishing strides, towards his design /Moves like a ghost." Then another rueful intuition of the moral status of what he is about to do: "Thou sure and firm-set earth, /Hear not my steps, which way they walk, for fear /The very stones prate of my whereabout, /And take the present horror from the time, /Which now suits with it." These moments of moral awareness and self-awareness lay a foundation for the tough stoic solidity to the final lines, "I go, and it is done; the bell invites me. / Hear it not, Duncan, for it is a knell, /That summons thee to heaven, or to hell."

Such are the conditions and the movements of Macbeth's mind at the crucial moment before the act. This kind of illumination of the processes of mind, feeling, and conscience that allows him to respond to the witches' temptation has, of course, been the project of the whole play.

Welles seems to all but reject this project, judging by his lack of interest in the order of the mental events in Macbeth's experience. He schedules the dagger speech early, well before the actual murder it leads to in Shakespeare, and in rearranging its elements – the apparition of the dagger, the speech to and about it, and the rejection of it as only an apparition – Welles demotes the hallucination from being the terrible last message Macbeth's moral imagination speaks to him, the most vividly realized, to being just another instance of his vacillating will. It isn't even clear that Welles knew what he was doing, for he retains in his cut version the beginning of Macbeth's coming to terms with the hallucination, "There's no such thing." In their original context these lines show that Macbeth has mastered his fear of the apparition and is ready to commit the murder, but in Welles's version it doesn't show anything clearly. It is when Macbeth then joins Lady Macbeth that Welles chooses to have him say, "We will proceed no further in this business" (I.vii.31), occasioning her brilliantly abusive and provocative attack on his will and manhood, which Welles presents almost complete. But if Macbeth has already said, "There's no such thing," it makes little sense for him to want to back out now. Welles has jumbled the order of mental events. The large elements of the action leading up to the murder are scattered around almost helter-skelter – and since Shakespeare's sequence has been abandoned, we forget about the issue of the ordering of Macbeth's emotions: his hesitations and hallucinations of conscience, his guilt, his susceptibility to Lady Macbeth's will, her scorn and her terrifying practicality. Bits and pieces of Shakespeare's language remain, so that the scene thrills again and again with brilliant disjunct flashes of feeling and meaning. But we usually call the drama of minute-by-minute sensation "melodrama."

Welles does another kind of rearranging in "If it were done, when 'tis done," the other great Macbeth soliloquy in the action leading to Duncan's murder:

> If it were done, when 'tis done, then 'twere well
> It were done quickly. If th' assassination
> Could trammel up the consequence, and catch
> With his surcease, success; that but this blow
> Might be the be-all and the end-all – here,
> But here, upon this bank and shoal of time,
> We'ld jump the life to come. But in these cases
> We still have judgment here, that we but teach
> Bloody instructions, which, being taught, return
> To plague th' inventor; this even-handed justice
> Commends th' ingredience of our poison'd chalice
> To our own lips. He's here in double trust:
> First, as I am his kinsman and his subject,
> Strong both against the deed; then, as his host,
> Who should against his murtherer shut the door,
> Not bear the knife myself. Besides, this Duncan
> Hath borne his faculties so meek, hath been
> So clear in his great office, that his virtues
> Will plead like angels, trumpet-tongu'd against
> The deep damnation of his taking-off;
> And pity, like a naked new-born babe,
> Striding the blast, or heaven's cherubin hors'd
> Upon the sightless couriers of the air,
> Shall blow the horrid deed in every eye,
> That tears shall drown the wind. I have no spur
> To prick the sides of my intent, but only
> Vaulting ambition, which o'erleaps itself,
> And falls on th' other –
> (I.vii.1–28)

Welles divides this in half, placing the second half (slightly altered) first, before Macbeth and Lady Macbeth listen to a prayer to Saint Michael (a Welles fabrication); the revised version of this part begins with another lame Welles fabrication, "King Duncan is my kinsman," then jumps to "he hath borne his faculties so meek," and continues as in the original to a revised version of the ending, which cuts "I have no spur" and what follows. This drops out and thus distorts important stages in Macbeth's thinking: his steady orderly naming of the pieties and obligations he ought to feel toward Duncan, and the terms in which he confesses his failure of will, so that something important is missing. In Shakespeare's version, Macbeth first weighs the crime in terms of practical and psychological economy rather than moral values – considering how the effects of the crime would play out in practical consequences rather than in feeling and conscience. This merges into listing and weighing the taboos that he would break if he murdered Duncan.[2] And then his thinking is invaded by a surge of feeling at the word "pity," which produces one of the most spectacular changes of tone in Shakespeare, as Macbeth's sudden imagination of the moral actuality of the crime overtakes and drowns out calculation, swelling until it fills his mind completely. The power and validity of these lines is governed by the structure of the whole speech, for were such high rhetoric to appear out of nowhere, with no lead-up, it could scarcely avoid bombast; nor does Welles entirely escape it. Yet he has timed his replacement of this semi-soliloquy effectively: Duncan has just entered his castle, the priest is leading his prayer, Macbeth and Lady Macbeth are holding themselves quietly to one side, not participating in the ritual but observing it respectfully. All this is well managed. But within a few lines we are hearing the extreme rhetoric about "pity, like a naked newborn babe," and Duncan's virtues pleading "like angels trumpet-tongu'd against/The deep damnation of his taking-off." It is too much, too soon.

These rearrangements can't have come from any considerable thinking about the play. In another instance, it must have been sheer inattention that led Welles to place right after the murder, with Lady Macbeth as Macbeth's only audience, a speech that in Shakespeare has a quite different tone and function:

> MACBETH: Had I but died an hour before this chance,
> I had liv'd a blessed time; for from this instant
> There's nothing serious in mortality:
> All is but toys: renown and grace is dead,
> The wine of life is drawn, and the mere lees
> Is left this vault to brag of.
> (II.iii.91–96)

In Welles's entirely misplaced version, this becomes Macbeth's despair at the death of Duncan, whereas in Shakespeare it is a PR handout Macbeth has cooked up for public consumption, as its phony tone makes perfectly clear. It is splendidly contrived for that purpose; its overripe falseness adds a new, unpleasant dimension to Macbeth's action, but this is not Macbeth's conscience speaking, and Welles must have been working very fast and carelessly to have thought it was. He also must not have known exactly what he was doing when he invented a new line for Macbeth (and of course for himself): "Leave the rest to me," he says, a pitifully colorless invention that intrudes a weak irony into the strong web of deep ironies that holds Shakespeare's scene together; the invented line also foolishly upstages Lady Macbeth's "you shall put/This night's great business into my dispatch" (I.v.67–68), and everything that goes with it, including the electrifyingly humanizing admission she voices as she waits outside the royal bedroom: "I laid their daggers ready,/He could not miss 'em. Had he not resembled/My father as he slept, I had done't" (II.ii.11–13). Welles bafflingly cut this last unmatchable stroke – it is beyond guessing what he thought he was achieving by these capricious depredations.

Yet one forgives some of even Welles's worst cuts in the light of his cinematic inventiveness. It is true that the dagger speech is matched on the screen by a glowing neon mirage – Special Effects, vintage 1948 – that just escapes being corny. But in the place of some of the cut material, Welles invented richly suggestive cinematic images and actions. There's a brilliant stroke where he had cut Lady Macbeth's speech to Macbeth during their first moments of thinking together about the murder. He makes the dialogue between the two of them parts of a large passage of idiomatic film language, which may persuade us not to grieve over some of the wild cuts he had made in Lady Macbeth's welcoming speech and the ensuing scene.

The arrival at Dunsinane Castle is played out in a rich montage in which two actions are intercut: Macbeth's eager, posthaste ride toward his castle and his wife, and Cawdor's slow, weary progress to the same destination – he is being dragged to Dunsinane for execution. In Shakespeare the execution is narrated by Malcolm, in a set piece containing a well-known line in praise of Cawdor's behavior: "Nothing in his life/Became him like the leaving it" (I.iv.7–8). Welles perhaps took his cue from this for his own image of Cawdor's approach to death.

The intercutting of the two actions begins at the end of Lady Macbeth's conjuration:

> Come, thick night,
> And pall thee in the dunnest smoke of hell,
> That my keen knife see not the wound it makes,
> Nor heaven peep through the blanket of the dark
> To cry, "Hold, hold!"
> (I.v.50–55)

On these words she faces away and the screen fills with swirling clouds and fog, "the dunnest smoke of hell," which when it lifts shows Macbeth riding hard on horseback. Jacques Ibert's music here sounds rather like formula music for fast riding in Hollywood Westerns, and it works well enough. But Macbeth's furious riding is interrupted, and the meaning of what we see next is uncertain. We look at foggy fields without knowing why, and when we hear what may be a dim drumbeat, we don't know what that is or means, either.

In the next scene we find out. As we draw closer, the sound clarifies into threatening regular drumbeats, and then we see them struck with impassive relish by two bare-chested men. This could be a general ceremonial tattoo, but the looks of the men, the violence of the drumbeats, and the general atmosphere suggest something more ominous. A small man (Macbeth's personal servant, Seyton) runs down a curving staircase from the castle into the courtyard of Dunsinane, and his movement directs our attention to entering soldiers, whom we recognize only when we see that they are dragging the Thane of Cawdor between their horses. Now we understand that the traitor is, in the traditional style, being drawn to execution, and we identify the drumming as part of the ceremony. We have seen Cawdor briefly before, long enough to be struck by the contrast between his delicate wasted features and the coarser faces of most of the soldiers. His face as he goes to death is gentle and weary, its thin exhausted lineaments seem especially highly bred. Taking their initial cue from Malcolm's: "Nothing in his life became him like the leaving it," Welles and the mute (and uncredited) performer who plays Cawdor collaborate in presenting his execution in a noble and pathetic mode.

The execution is a system of organized brutality. Welles lays the structure of the system out through clear actions and gestures on the part of all the characters, choreographing all the actions legibly, so that the frame of the screen becomes, in an effect Welles always likes, a space completely charged with energy and meaning. Cawdor is pushed up toward the top of the stairs of execution, which is also the top of the screen, bringing the violent event close to us, intruding it into our consciousness and almost threatening us physically; then, at the bottom of the stairs, which is also the bottom of the frame of the screen, another shirtless muscular man strides forward toward us, climbing briskly and purposefully, and intrusively, up the hill beside the stairs; as he swings his arms and upper body limberly in an exhibition of physical assurance, his idiosyncratic gait and bearing suggest that he has a quite special purpose; when he enters the same frame as the huge executioner's axe, we realize who he is. There follows yet another appearance of the Holy Father (Alan Napier) whom we have already seen too often (Welles changed Shakespeare's Ross into a priest, probably in order to argue his theory that the witches were thought in the culture of Macbeth's time to be the servants of Satan, the deadly enemies of the newly emerging Christendom); the priest begins to officiate as leader of the ceremony, climbing to the top of the hill of execution, where he is joined by the executioner; Cawdor is pushed up more tightly into the top frame, with the priest and the executioner; his head is forced brutally down on what we now identify as the rock of execution, and the axe falls.

Just at this point, Welles intercuts the action of the execution with Macbeth's arrival at the castle, leaping from his horse and hastening toward Lady Macbeth in the middle of the courtyard; he moves toward her; the animal energy and desire strikingly different from the movements of all involved in the execution; meanwhile, the violence of the execution is now being connected, in an irony too rich and too elusive to paraphrase, with the violence we know Macbeth to be considering. He embraces Lady Macbeth in a long kiss, with the unmistakable passion of physical hunger and need; she gives herself fully. Their enactment of the passionate life of the senses and the blood occurs – as by now we expect – just as the great axe falls on Cawdor's neck and the drumming simultaneously stops. The two actions – Macbeth's and Lady Macbeth's kiss of love and ambition and life hunger, and the weary, humiliated Cawdor's acceptance of death – pull against each other, but the Macbeths' act of life boasts its superiority. For a moment after the execution, Macbeth and Lady Macbeth remain, in separation but together, poised, aware of what's happening and perhaps taking its measure; then Lady Macbeth begins to plan the murder she takes for granted they are going to attempt.

The passion of their embrace yields a formidable image of the fullness of their sexual communication, but it also alerts us to look for the strains that will test them, especially Lady Macbeth, who has already, in "unsex me here," begun her terrifying exploration of the boundaries of her nature. The strong sexual force between the two carries them, on the rising action of the play, straight through to Macbeth's plan for the murder of Banquo, when, in an excruciating irony, Shakespeare has Macbeth try, with sickeningly mistimed considerateness, to keep Lady Macbeth from the anxiety of knowing his dark plan; this act of love from Macbeth leads, in a terrible geometry, straight to their bleak estrangement afterward.

After the embrace, Lady Macbeth greets Macbeth by his new title and refers glancingly to his future title of king; her lines thrill with shared excitement – in Jeanette Nolan's performance she seems to intertwine her breath with his:

> Thy letters have transported me beyond
> This ignorant present, and I feel now
> The future in the instant.
> (I.v.57–59)

Her excited expectation seeks to quiet Macbeth's anxiety; his ambition is always complicated by doubt, her practical energy always free from scruple.

And now Welles begins an astonishing rearrangement of the text. Here is Shakespeare's version:

> MACBETH: My dearest love,
> Duncan comes here to-night.
> LADY MACBETH: And when goes hence?
> MACBETH: To-morrow, as he purposes.
> LADY MACBETH: O, never
> Shall sun that morrow see!
> Your face, my thane, is as a book, where men
> May read strange matters. To beguile the time,
> Look like the time; bear welcome in your eye,
> Your hand, your tongue; look like th' innocent flower,
> But be the serpent under't. He that's coming
> Must be provided for; and you shall put
> This night's great business into my dispatch,
> Which shall to all our nights and days to come
> Give solely sovereign sway and masterdom.
> MACBETH: We will speak further.
> (I.v.58–71)

And here is Welles's version:

> MACBETH: My dearest love,
> Duncan comes here to-night.
> LADY MACBETH: And when goes hence?
> MACBETH: Tomorrow, as he purposes.
> LADY MACBETH: He that's coming
> Must be provided for;
> MACBETH: We will speak further.
> LADY MACBETH: Put this night's business into my dispatch.

Perhaps only a youthfully self-assured genius would have had the nerve, or whatever it took, to blue-pencil Lady Macbeth's "O, never/Shall sun

"Innocent of the knowledge, dearest chuck," says Macbeth to his Lady (Jeanette Nolan). He's just arranged the murder of Banquo, but he's not – "with sickeningly mistimed considerateness" – telling her about it. (Photo courtesy of Photofest)

that morrow see!" – a coup de théâtre of maximum brilliance in itself and solidly prepared for. The preceding dialogue in Welles's version feeds so exactly into the exulting threat that Welles almost seems to have missed the point of the psychological complexity in Shakespeare's text. Of course he didn't miss it; he had another point to make, which as it happened worked out quite marvelously. When he substituted for the great theatrical cry Lady Macbeth's few unprepossessing words from a bit later in the speech, "He that's coming/Must be provided for," he was vindicated in the event, and must have known he would be, by what Nolan could make out of these words. She turns that simple declarative into an intensely careful (but also oddly tender) explanation, sharing her understanding with him, while also giving him orders. Duncan is to be provided for by being killed, that's the huge irony of her words, of course; but her solicitousness, her making sure Macbeth understands, her confiding smile, all these seek to touch Macbeth so closely and sensuously that she seems almost to approach the obscene. Macbeth speaks his next line while turning his face toward us, partly avoiding the issue, partly trying to assume command: "We will speak further." And Nolan's searching tone in her answer, "Put this night's business into my dispatch," proves her capable indeed of taking all the unimaginable complexities and eventualities of the murder "into her dispatch." Her thrilling smile as she makes this promise asks Macbeth to take her loyalty and passion for granted – and passion is an absolute imperative for both of them. She seems to be reasoning that if by temperament he is a man who needs to have someone take care of everything, whatever the scope of "everything" might turn out to be, it is not because of cowardice or incompetence on his part but because of the incapacitating hesitations and doubts of the troubled nature she knows well – from the depths of which he later on speaks to her with poignant frankness:

> the affliction of these terrible dreams
> That shake us nightly. Better be with the dead,
> Whom we, to gain our peace, have sent to peace,
> Than on the torture of the mind to lie
> In restless ecstasy.
> (III.ii.18–22)

After all of Welles's cutting, a couple of lines were left over that he wanted to save, rightly, since they act out the practicality that Lady Macbeth tries to teach Macbeth, in small ways as well as in such monumental outbursts as "Why did you bring these daggers from the place?/They must lie there." Welles extracted the lines he wanted to keep from the speech and set them apart by themselves for emphasis:

> Your face, my thane, is as a book, where men
> May read strange matters. To beguile the time,
> Look like the time; bear welcome in your eye,
> Your hand, your tongue; look like th' innocent flower,
> But be the serpent under't.
> (I.v.62–66)

In Welles's film, these lines are what Lady Macbeth is saying during the first of the important series of two-shots of Macbeth and Lady Macbeth, which, among other structural devices, bind the sequence together. The two are watching the entry of the king's retinue into their castle, standing on the sidelines of the procession; though no one is within listening range,

Nolan plays the scene almost sotto voce; her vocal wariness corresponds to her stylized facial performance of correctness in formal attitude and tone; she is performing to deceive watchers even when no watcher is near, educating Macbeth in the duplicity she is recommending. When she rebukes his naïve transparency, she calls him, "My thane," ironically and with almost mocking condescension, but her gleaming high satirical smile and the boldly provocative, extravagantly legible play of her eyes and lashes, enter into collusion with him. The lesson she offers her pupil-husband comes from her intelligent, practical temperament; and her super-articulation italicizes and dramatizes the lesson – Nolan utters a never-before-heard voicing of "tongue," which an almost stuttered "t" makes into a prominent phonetic event, as is the operatic drop with the strongly sculpted vowels and consonants in "be" and "serpent" and the consciously sinister elegance of the long-drawn-out first syllable of "serpent." The speech acts out her authority and self-command in its composure and oddity, while her explicit manipulation of her features, her eyes and makeup, compose a bravura performance of deceitfulness for Macbeth's education.

There's a faint undercurrent of wit in another two-shot. As the man of God begins a tiresome drone to Saint Michael, coercing everybody into the mood and act of prayer and eventually into a ludicrous Sunday-school confessional antiphony that is worlds away from what one imagines as Shakespeare's taste ("Dost thou swear to reject Satan and all his works?" "I do") repeated earnestly by everybody from Duncan on down – during all this, only one person seems to resist the coercion, though Lady Macbeth performs the appearance of piety impeccably. She looks down with an archly mimicked, an almost wittily satirized reverence and humility, while at her side Macbeth (susceptible to spiritual promptings as she is not) keeps his eyes open and then uses the occasion to speak the second half of the "If it were done when 'tis done" soliloquy.

At the end of that speech, Welles effectively complicates our experience of the soliloquy by having Lady Macbeth come down the stairs toward Macbeth while he is still speaking. When she reaches him, Welles gives us a two-shot of them from the side; they are in a kind of embrace, with Lady Macbeth leaning closely into his body as she makes her triumphant report about having drugged Duncan's bodyguards:

> When in swinish sleep
> Their drenched natures lie as in a death,
> What cannot you and I perform upon
> Th' unguarded Duncan? what not put upon

His spungy officers, who shall bear the guilt
Of our great quell?
MACBETH: Bring forth men-children only!
For thy undaunted mettle should compose
Nothing but males.
(I.vii.67–74)

Nolan acknowledges the tribute in an audacious invention. She finds a miraculously well-judged modern tone – a deep transformation of a flirtatious 'Oh, you!' – which her recklessness instills with playful sexual promise, all without violating the consistency of manners and behavior she has been following.

This is only the most audacious of the many such strokes in Nolan's and Welles's performances; the mutuality with which they work well together constitutes the film's special mode and its excellence. Here finally is the sufficient answer to our troubling worries about Welles's cuts and rearrangements. They matter certainly; they matter a lot, and if one remembers the important passages that are missing, one regrets the loss immensely. When we forget about these cuts and rearrangements, which happens again and again, it is sometimes through the operation of that optical illusion already described. But more important it happens because we are drawn to the film's representation of a human action that is so deeply interesting that it completely fills our attention. When we realize and respond to the depth and power of Welles and Nolan's relationship, full of richly imagined detail on the one hand, grounded in large understandings and intuitions on the other, then all cavils about Welles's reckless cuts sink into unimportance.

When we are in tune with the film's special excellence, the insufficiencies of its cheap set and costumes also sink away, for now we are in the mood to see and appreciate what Welles has achieved with his minimal resources. In a thoroughly idiomatic passage of cinematic art and method, Welles's use of depth cinematography, and of the structure of the set itself, brilliantly clarifies what is going on between Macbeth and Lady Macbeth, which is of course what we want most to see. After Duncan calls his new Thane of Cawdor to him, for thanks and congratulations, he does the same with Banquo (Edgar Barrier); we next see Macbeth walking toward the rear wall, and deep focus makes it a pleasure, a kind of treat, to see so clearly the moment when Lady Macbeth, at some distance, begins to come toward him; we see her next more closely in a sharper-edged image; when they meet we see that she is carrying a large flask, which she hands him to hold while she corrupts it with a drug from an elegant vial. It is thrilling to see her act out what she has so confidently promised. (Welles may have picked up the flavor of this moment from the poisonings of Eisenstein's *Ivan the Terrible;* Lady Macbeth's eyes gleaming in the dark also recall Eisenstein, and Ibert's music for this action is also somewhat reminiscent of Prokofiev's for Ekaterina's poisoning.) Now Duncan, moving slowly up the staircase, toward the top of the wall, and then walking along the wall to his bedchamber, speaks the supreme and almost unbearably ironic lines (I.vi.4–6) that praise Dunsinane Castle as the haunt of the "temple-haunting martlet," the bird that shows that "heaven's breath smells / Wooingly" wherever it appears – in this case the martlet's "lov'd mansionry" is gracing what is soon to be a charnel house. Welles's inclusion of these purely "descriptive" lines might be puzzling in the light of his propensity to cut, were it not that he soon shows himself to be preparing another idiomatic drama of cinema. While Duncan is celebrating this augury of grace, Lady Macbeth begins a heroic run up the stairs to overtake Duncan's servants and give them the drugged flask. We easily follow her movement – another benefit of deep focus – and in fact we seem to see more than we possibly could see. Moving the terrible action forward is Lady Macbeth's intention in this scene as always, but her speed and agility in running up the steep stairs is the sort of unexpected and vividly enacted detail that gives freshness to the film's entire imagining of the play.

A bit later, when Lady Macbeth is waiting down at our level for Macbeth to return from committing the murder, deep focus keeps the high wall that leads to Duncan's bedchamber a solid fact for us, while from behind Lady Macbeth we watch her watching, in the foreground both of the physical space and of our attention; when Macbeth appears high on that wall, we see him distinctly, far away though he is, and again the scene gets power and we get special pleasure from the unexpected clarity of our vision, the sensation of seeing so distinctly the connection between Macbeth and his wife. At such moments all murmurings against the drab mud shapes that try so pitifully to represent castles and battlements cease, for Welles has plotted and photographed the action in and upon this mud castle so clearly that our attention is entirely commanded by it.

The tawdry, meager mud structure representing Dunsinane Castle is reminiscent of the "experimental" sets in the Little Theatre movement of the thirties, but eventually one notices how often and how inventively Welles has escaped these limitations. The castle erected on the set at the

Universal Studios was made out of the same papier-mâché as the whole set, whether or not it claims to represent a stone staircase, curving sharply upward; also a broad, flat top of a battlement, which later serves as a broad corridor leading to Duncan's bedchamber. Both staircase and wall are in the last analysis efficiently designed playing spaces that get fully explored and brought to life by the action. Usually we see them from a distance, to give maximum play to the deep focus that Welles at this stage of his career has learned how to use with flexibility and discretion, with ample meaning and no sense of mere display. In the murder sequence, Lady Macbeth, close to us during the murder, is alarmed by something Macbeth has done or failed to do, sure that something has gone badly wrong; then, far away, on the high wall, Macbeth himself emerges; we see him clearly, and we see the two of them clearly in the same frame. In a hundred other ways Welles has crowded this unlovely mud structure with the purposes and anxieties of the great characters, their energy, tension, fear, doubt, watchfulness.

These brilliant uses of the medium of film throughout *Macbeth* go a long way to compensate for Welles's rearrangements of Shakespeare's text. But what the film most resoundingly achieves is simpler, more old-fashioned, more treasurable than this suggests: the depth and freshness with which Welles and Nolan understand, feel, invent, and project their roles, and the close responsiveness of interaction with which they play together.

Macbeth has every kind of power a play can have, and everybody agrees that the relationship between Macbeth and Lady Macbeth is the source and center of that power. But Welles's *Macbeth* is distinctly a film – that is, it is composed in a medium ideally, idiomatically, equipped to convey immediate intuitive knowledge of the identities and relationships of human beings and to bring us into the most painful and valuable closeness with them. The congruence of matter and medium possible in a film version of Shakespeare's *Macbeth* is what all the participants in Welles's *Macbeth* must have been in tune with instinctively, and it is what they achieved. This is supremely true of Welles as director and actor, and of Nolan as actor, working together in this intuitive harmony.

Instinctively, intuitively – those are the keynotes. In the full-bodied openness and spontaneity of Welles's and Nolan's gestures, body movements, facial expressions, one catches the spirit that must have governed Welles's whole troupe in the staged version of the play he directed in Salt Lake City, which he used as rehearsal for the film which he then, in record time, shot on the Republic Pictures lot.

Lady Macbeth (Nolan) watches the new king with growing alarm, as he falls apart in front of his subjects; between them is Lady Macduff (Peggy Webber). (Photo courtesy of Photofest)

Othello

With *Journey into Fear* (1942) and *The Stranger* (1946) the irregularity of the second half of Welles's career had begun to emerge. In public reputation he remained the brilliant master of *Citizen Kane* throughout his life, but even that unequivocal masterpiece had originally come to the world in a cloud of speculations, rumors, threats of vendetta, and an actual vendetta. As for *The Magnificent Ambersons,* only the deepest insiders were aware of the vandalism visited on this film, to some large extent due to carelessness, recklessness, ignorance, and too much hopefulness on the part of Welles himself. When part of the true story of what had happened to *The Magnificent Ambersons* came out, Welles's work was ever afterward accompanied by stories behind the story, anecdotes, speculation, and outrage about the miserable conditions under which the work had been accomplished and in many respects very brilliantly accomplished. This penumbra of gossip wasn't at all merely idle nor was it always mean-spirited; the new film was often generously interpreted in terms of the handicaps under which it had been made. Indeed, this atmosphere was in some respects an enviable dramatic light for a brilliant maverick to be working in, and it goes without saying that Welles took every advantage of it. His special audience, and a considerable part of the general audience, was in sympathy with him, and the heroic drama of this genius fighting for his individuality against the conventionality, venality, timidity, and outright dishonesty of Hollywood lay close to the heart of much thinking about the future of film art in America during the forties and fifties – not the least of Welles's greatness was to have kept that drama of the artist versus the studio alive by keeping himself constantly in the middle of it and in front of the public.

It wasn't easy to take the measure of each of Welles's films in the middle of this hubbub, which in some cases distracted attention from the films themselves and led to confusion about their value. *Othello* is for me the most interesting and ambiguous case in this respect.

My first glimpse of *Othello* made it seem almost thrillingly handsome, and pointed to the "look" of the film – the structure, tone, and texture of the cinematography – as the film's central quality and excellence. My memory of the altogether less handsome use of the medium in *Macbeth* set the new *Othello* on a golden pedestal. The shabby surface of *Macbeth* had already disturbed and bothered me because in *Citizen Kane* and *The Magnificent Ambersons* I had taken such pleasure in the dazzlingly ripened fruits of the wunderkind's widely reported apprenticeship in film: his research into the films of the past, in particular the black-and-white films that he had been absorbing in the crash course he was giving himself in European, particularly German, cinema of the twenties and thirties. Whatever the origin of the visual splendor of *Citizen Kane* and *The Magnificent Ambersons,* the look of *Macbeth* came as a shocking disappointment. It's possible now to regard the look of *Macbeth* more calmly, as a decent if rather provincial and certainly ill-made approximation of and tribute to the rich UFA tone, but at first the cheapness of the materials out of which décor and costumes had been fashioned, and the inexpertise with which they were being displayed, seemed merely pitiful. Contemplating the homely dowdiness of sets and costumes in *Macbeth,* the walls of mud, the moldy bearskin robes, the tusked helmets on loan from some high-school-drama wardrobe, the banal imagery of the witches' swirling clouds of evil – looking at all this, it was depressing to see that a major aspect of the Welles enterprise was in poor shape, for one remembered the art work as one of the distinct glories of the enterprise. Welles was now working at Republic Pictures, a B-picture and cowboy specialty house of deliberately circumscribed resources, with costumes limited in expense and variety and in whole groups of items ordinarily found in the wardrobe of Hollywood, where the resources might not in some cases have the distinction of the art work at UFA, but in many cases did have exactly that distinction, since so many of them were in the control of refugees from the German studios. Welles had had unusual license in budget with both *Citizen Kane* and *The Magnificent Ambersons,* not without some complications, of course, but the budget of *Macbeth* at Republic was realistically scheduled and overseen, and Welles seemed aware of responsibilities and imaginative about how to fulfill them without quarreling.

He must have learned something from the sobering experience with the poverty-stricken *Macbeth,* but the later and handsomer *Othello* is in fact less successful than the earlier film, both as film and as Shakespeare. Rather surprisingly, a chief weakness in *Othello* is in its "look," surprising because it was the poverty-stricken décor of *Macbeth* that had come in for abuse, in the present discussion for instance. My view of the *Othello* has changed, rather embarrassingly so, for it was once a decided favorite of mine among Welles's work and has since lost much of its hold on me. I saw it soon after *Macbeth,* and at first my memory of the drab, impoverished look of that film was so fresh in my memory that it threw the brilliant black and white of *Othello* into high relief. I still remember rolling those splendid, sumptuous images over and over on my visual palate – not that I had anything like the connoisseurship this implies, but that I much wanted to have it and sought out occasions to practice: *Othello* offered a prime opportunity. The boldness of Welles's black-and-white contrasts registered on me as living splendor. I hadn't yet seen Venice or any Italian locale, so I wasn't moved one way or another by memory – didn't then feel irritated at what has come to seem touristic imagery. I recognized and admired the Ducal Palace but hadn't seen it either in life or too often in art not to be impressed by the mere sight of it. My main response to *Othello,* I confess, was a sort of naïve pleasure and pride that our young American Welles had made something not only so handsome but so effectively *competitive* with the great masters of cinema – with Eisenstein, for instance, who then formed my idea of world-class cinema. And the films of Eisenstein were in fact not uninvolved with this *Othello.*

Later experiences with *Othello* have unexpectedly brought dissatisfaction with the "look" of a film that had given such pleasure in that regard before. By the time he began *Othello* in 1949, Welles had lost all regular relations with the large, experienced art departments of film studios, and this may have been one of his reasons for filming *Othello* on location, as it were, in real places that resembled insofar as possible the fictive places where Shakespeare's action takes place. He toured southern Europe and North Africa, in memory and in actuality, looking for architectural images by which to represent Venice and Cyprus in the film, and he did in fact find buildings, squares, walls, parapets that suited the play and the photographic frame in which he was planning to install his images; for the most part he succeeded in matching the distinctive architectural identity of the sites he chose with the compositions of light and dark he planned for his cinematography.

Yet when one actually sees *Othello,* and when the grand roll of these great buildings gradually unfurls in the background of the action, a sense of overintentionality develops and then becomes wearying, and the look for the film, handsome at first, goes wrong in a direction opposite from the one taken in *Macbeth* – not toward expressionistic drabness but toward banal and conventional beauty, middlebrow luxury art-book richness and smoothness, which in turn soon brings to mind the images of commercial Venetian tourist posters. Fortunately, this is not always the case. When Desdemona (Suzanne Cloutier) goes to the Senate chamber to support Othello as he answers Brabantio's charges of having bewitched and abducted her, she hastens through one of the long colonnaded loggias of the actual Ducal Palace in Venice, and this is acceptable – for it is a generic loggia, so to speak, the essence of loggia, without the off-putting specificity of any actual place. But when Brabantio is discovered to live not in a generic Venetian palazzo but in the Palazzo Contarini-Bovolo, a distinctive Venetian building that we know from guidebooks and our own tourism, this doesn't work, for this palazzo is also the site of still another well-known Venetian tourist monument, the Renaissance spiral staircase called the Scala di Bovolo, a marvelous treasure too distinctive to be used as if it were merely vernacular Venetian architectural imagery. Welles easily makes the Scala di Bovolo look beautiful in the film, but its specificity, whether or not we recognize it, hampers its usefulness as a locus of action. Even if we don't find ourselves saying, 'Look, isn't that the Scala di Bovolo they're coming down!', we are looking at a readily identifiable building, and such recognition, perhaps pleasant in itself, is detrimental to the illusion the film is trying to create, for we seem to be watching a travelogue about Venice rather than Shakespeare's drama. When Desdemona goes to marry Othello, she logically leaves by way of this beautiful staircase, which is after all located in the building where she supposedly lives; and she leaves so quickly that the glimpses of the Bovolo don't dis-

One of the loggias in Welles's *Othello*. Suzanne Cloutier in foreground, with Welles in blackface behind. (Photo courtesy of Photofest)

tract from the action at this point. But later, after Iago has told Brabantio of the marriage and Brabantio has waked his household to check the report, his servants clatter noisily down this very staircase to the obtrusive sound of an overrecorded harpsichord, and the drama of Desdemona and Brabantio evaporates as Welles's exploitation of this site becomes obtrusive. Later on, he loses all discretion when, without a pretense of dramatic motive, he has us suddenly look down from above on the much too well-known bronze figures that strike the clock at the edge of Piazza San Marco; there is a gorgeously romantic vision of San Giorgio in the distance, to be sure, but this is calendar art rather than drama.

A different kind of inappropriateness weakens the scenes between Iago and Roderigo in the public baths. A well-known anecdote reports that these were the first scenes Welles shot and that they were shot first for an unusual reason – none of the costumes had yet arrived, and Welles decided that the bare skins of the naked actors could serve as sufficient costuming for scenes taking place in the baths. In fact they do, and all seems well; but soon there comes an overload of visual activity when the pillars in the scene turn out to be the foundation of a large Venetian building, the floor of which is ankle deep in water, logically enough for these baths perhaps, but leading to far too much entertaining splashing about when the characters move. The noisy Venetian décor has become an object of interest in itself, distracting attention from whatever action is going on within it. When this décor serves for other actions, still flooded with splashing water, we seem to be returning not because this is the appropriate décor for the next action but because Welles wants to repeat a charming and entertaining special cinematic effect. It's an innocuous instance of Welles's theatrical and performing art and it takes place harmlessly long before the tensions and stresses of the drama are in play, but the picturesque distraction nevertheless dilutes whatever drama might be building, and by the end of the film there have been too many charming diversions and too few serious nontheatrical dramatic expositions.

The whole film opens with a distraction on a far larger scale and in a different key – a set piece that asks for real respect and offers real power: the rich and solemn funeral procession for Othello and Desdemona. Their faces are veiled in dark but almost transparent netting that makes an exciting textural impact, and they are carried on biers by cloaked and hooded figures and escorted by clerics. The procession doesn't derive from Shakespeare and doesn't claim to, nor does it really suit Shakespeare's tone about these characters and their fate, which is far more ambiguous than what emerges from such a one-dimensionally heroic celebration. But the boldness of the visual images easily took the day the first time I saw the film. If it comes from any one particular source, Welles's jet-black cortege, silhouetted against brooding clouds, has less to do with Shakespeare's play than with the imagery of Eisenstein's famed *Alexander Nevsky* and the then-recently released (U.S., 1947) *Ivan the Terrible,* imagery inscribed on the screen by huge processions of the Russian people through meadows and on palace walls. The visual reminiscence delighted me because it showed that Welles, like the rest of the world, was as impressed by Eisenstein's images as I was, and that he had studied them fully. They are certainly worth study and worth imitating but not on every occasion, and the grand conventional heroics that open Welles's *Othello* testify less to Welles's attitude toward Shakespeare's hero and heroine than to his own noble intentions and high-toned sentiments. All is overblown – pompous meanings are enunciated with grandiloquence, then are heavily underlined by superaudible music in which the piano is emphatically foregrounded as a loud percussion instrument in a knowing pseudomodern manner, while an unsponsored chorus is wailing in the cellarage. We are not only in a different world from the gloomy opening of *Citizen Kane,* but we are dealing with a far cruder taste, handsome as the result may be. The half-parodic opening of *Citizen Kane* was enlivened with wit and intelligence by Bernard Herrmann's playful shiftings of his ominous tone, all suitable to the shifting tones and meanings of the material of *Citizen Kane,* and all adding to those meanings; but the opening funeral procession in *Othello* is all in one key, and its solemnity comes through as pomposity, even while we admire beautiful moments of the cinematography – the seductive grace of Desdemona's bier swimming in front of the camera, for instance.

Just before it gets too lugubrious, Welles shrewdly intercuts the funeral with a more dynamic line of action, different in imagery and tone, written in a more intense calligraphy – the punishment of Iago, who after the adagio of the funeral procession, is suddenly, with many jolts, irregularly snapped, pulled, jerked, yanked through the crowd, very fast, held by a rope tight around his neck, shoved into a great iron cage, and immediately swung aloft near the battlements. It is our first glimpse of Iago's face in the film, and Micheál Mac Liammóir's finest moment. Through the bars of this personal prison, he quietly and with dispassionate intelligence studies the world he has ruined. The dazzling high-contrast black-and-white cinematography makes this cage visually shocking in the glare of the Italian sun, and I was riveted by it when I first saw it, seized both by the idea of such a punishment, new to me, and by the startling impact of its realization. The power, originality, and flair of the concept itself are still alive, still impressive signs of the director's wide and resourceful learning and invention. I remember later finding a scene in Marlowe's *Tamburlaine,* in which the all-heroic Tamburlaine keeps Bazajeth, one of the many rulers he has conquered, by his side in a cage. But the dynamics of what Welles has put into action – the thrilling swing aloft, the compacted contrast of the tight close-up of Iago's face and the ranging spectacle of the whole torture – these in themselves make up an unforgettable drama of retribution.

Yet beginning *Othello* with this funeral is like choosing to wear a heavy, unwieldy costume throughout a play of great physical activity, and this is a surprising misjudgment from Welles. As we have seen often and will see again, he was a great wearer of costumes, and for the most part a remarkably canny one, who knew what would work, whom one doesn't imagine choosing a costume with implications too heavy to carry. But the monumental style of the funeral echoes throughout the film, and one cannot escape thinking that its main cause is the self-promotion of Welles himself, choosing large styles to suit his large ambitions for his subject.

Welles's Othello inevitably resembles his Macbeth in height and bulk, and there is straightforward and effective eloquence in both performances. His distinctive voice (which indeed ties together all the roles he played in his entire career) makes for particularly audible unity and coherence when he is speaking Shakespeare's language. All this is Welles's familiar self-presentation, but if we expect *Othello* to present itself brilliantly for our applause, the result turns out to lack most of the infectious energy that usually makes Welles's theatrical self-consciousness not only acceptable but enjoyable and meaningful.

Othello, which came four years after *Macbeth* and was made in entirely different circumstances, has a far richer and smoother cinematographic texture but is also less deeply and personally felt, as if it had been guided by a more conventional and public motive. The alert directing intelligence so vividly present in *Macbeth* is hardly visible in *Othello.* Even though the combination of funeral cortege and caged Iago is impressive, we miss the skill with which the double-action montage of the execution of Cawdor and Macbeth's arrival at Dunsinane is managed. Welles mismanages rather badly another interlocked sequence of events in *Othello,* Iago's plot against Cassio (II.iii). Iago begins the action by persuading Cassio (Michael Laurence), a bad drinker, to drink too much, and then prompts Roderigo (Robert Coote) to insult the tipsy Cassio. He had told Montano (Jean Davis), onetime governor of Cyprus, that Cassio is a habitual drunkard, indirectly prompting Montano to intervene when Cassio attacks Roderigo; when Cassio in turn attacks Montano himself, that action generates the general melee that Iago loudly names a mutiny, arousing Othello from his marriage bed to calm things down. Eventually Othello cashiers Cassio, for it was on his watch that the disturbance took place. When Iago next advises Cassio to ask Desdemona to intercede for him with Othello to get his post back, Iago's plot is in full operation. This is an obviously important sequence, for although Iago has already confessed himself a villain in one of those direct addresses to the audience that Shakespeare loves and uses so adroitly, our sense of Iago's villainy is significantly enlarged and intensified as we watch this plot taking shape. In order for that to happen, we must understand exactly what is going on, but, through carelessness or laziness, Welles slightly blurs this action so that we don't quite understand precisely what is happening. It is conceivable that Welles himself hadn't really, strictly speaking, worked it out; he certainly didn't appreciate how well his superexpert colleague Shakespeare had put the thing together. Cassio at first refuses Iago's invitation to drink because he knows he can't hold his liquor, then consents to drink one stoup of wine as a courtesy to Iago, but refuses to continue; Iago gets him to drink more with an ingenious invention – "here without are a brace of Cyprus gallants that would fain have a measure to the health of black Othello," and Cassio gives in because the idea is hard to turn down diplomatically: "I'll do't, but it dislikes me." As we watch this play itself out, the whole point of this kind of dramaturgy is that we see the sequence of events very clearly, in order to admire how exactly Iago has planned it, using accurate knowledge of how the people he knows think and act. Since Cassio is wary of drink, there has to be a good reason for him to drink so much that he gets drunk; Iago's invention of the "gallants" supplies that good reason and also shows us Iago's easy mastery of invention. But in the Welles *Othello,* we don't hear the details of Iago's plot clearly enough, so the Cyprus gallants don't register solidly on our consciousness, and we don't quite catch Iago's device for getting Cassio to drink some more. Many other pieces of the logic of Iago's plot are also blurred in the film.

The careful procedures of the studios (with continuity of staff and storyboards and so on) would have handled this sort of thing capably as a routine task, and one thinks of Welles as rejecting good-boy carefulness yet not taking the pains to make his own more spontaneous methods really work. There's a sense partly of sloppiness, partly of making do with what the money buys but in the absence of money.

Welles's choice to cast his old friend and mentor Mac Liammóir as Iago was natural and generous, and Welles must have hoped to acquire in him a major determinant of the film's tone and style and, perhaps more important, the unifier of both tone and style. Although they hadn't worked together often since Welles's apprenticeship, those early experiences had established an intricate rapport; they had conversed often and continuously and had maintained detailed correspondence, both written and verbal, about the theater and about Shakespeare. They seemed hand in glove, and Welles's invention for Iago's first appearance is masterly, as we have seen. Welles's vision of Iago in the cage is one of the bold strokes of the film, a keynote in its style and a virtual proof of Welles's powerful invention. But Mac Liammóir's general reading of Iago is far from as successful – it's in the mode of the winnowed, tired, scornful wit of English drawing-room comedy, a decision that takes the reading of the whole play down a path that has less to do with traditions and conventions of standard English theater, and more to do with the mannerisms of Anglo-Irish acting, which exert their narrowing and almost debilitating effect on the scope of the play's dramatic and psychological identity.

With Micheál Mac Liammóir as Iago. (Photo courtesy of Photofest)

The only respite from this tone comes in the dialogue between Othello and Iago about the word "honest," a scene that chances also to be perhaps the best in the film, and even in the play. Here one may see why Welles needed Mac Liammóir. The action of the scene is Iago's probing, echoing antiphony on the word "honest" in III.iii. His aim is to begin Othello's temptation into jealousy. Twice, with feline, considerate cruelty, he probes: "I see this hath a little dash'd your spirits," to which Othello answers, not strongly, "Not a jot, not a jot"; then soon afterward, "My Lord, I see y' re moved." This is followed by the pitifully weak, almost mute response, "No, not much mov'd." It would be a great scene with its interchanges, even if it were played in a stationary format; but that would be immeasurably less effective than what Welles and Mac Liammóir achieve by adding the ingredient of their motion, at a fast almost military clip, as they round the watch – it makes one think that *Othello* would be worth making as a film if only for the dramatic intensity generated when this sly antiphonal dialogue is stretched out over the walking of the huge space that Welles has dared to use.

Cloutier's Desdemona. (Photo courtesy of Photofest)

Suzanne Cloutier's Desdemona, which has seemed inadequate to some critics, is one clear success in the film, and a beautiful achievement. It is a small performance; neither her conception of the character, nor her physical identity, nor the performance itself can match the size, strength, and revelatory power of Nolan's Lady Macbeth. And it is true too that she somewhat lacks presence, physical and temperamental, sometimes to a critical degree, as those will feel who remember the young Maggie Smith's Desdemona in the 1965 film with Laurence Olivier– a beautifully grave performance caught just before Smith's great talent and training had begun its rapid degeneration into the actressy Royal Academy mannerisms and tricks of forced charm out of which she constructed her roles during much of the rest of her career. In the Olivier film, Smith's movingly young, proud, tender uprightness became expressive in itself, creating an image of Desdemona's strength and serenity that speaks for itself beyond the words. Cloutier lacks the authority of Smith's stature, but her slightness makes its own poignant meanings powerful, particularly when seen so often next to Welles's bulk. This quiet Desdemona has a spirit that glows steadily from her countenance – open, grave, still, wondering, her face holding the light almost magically long as she submits quietly and with confidence to our gaze; she is at peace at intense moments, holding the dramatic situation steady, thereby giving us the right point of view on Othello's hysteria. She is mysteriously unhysterical herself in her agonizing request that Othello not kill her. Her line reading, which may reflect her complex cultural background in its elegant and original intonation, may have been one reason why Welles was eager to use her. He must have relished her frightened but steady answers to Othello's hysterical demands about the handkerchief (III.iv), answers that remain sweet and strong, without shrillness: "It is not lost. But what an if it were?" And when she answers Othello's thundering "Fetch't, let me see't," her calm trust in her own good faith seems an index to her integrity while it makes the dramatic situation almost agonizing: "Why, so I can, sir; but I will not now./This is a trick to put me from my suit./Pray you let Cassio be receiv'd again." In all this one feels one is seeing her own inspiration, her performance, and her identity, unimpeded by the bravura of her director's more flamboyant ego. This quiet Desdemona is Cloutier's success, not world-shaking but clear and deep.

The expensive glow of *Othello,* in relation to the success of the Desdemona, was reassuring. *Othello* seemed visually exciting – the Welles eye was functioning again. But in a later view, the film has gradually diminished into being only a capable moment-by-moment translation of the play, never rising into the independent life and conviction that *Macbeth* reached when the relation between Welles and Jeanette Nolan took fire. The series of intelligent and tasteful effects and meanings that makes up the substance of *Othello* isn't the same thing as interesting art.

Chimes at Midnight

Welles had been thinking about and imagining Shakespeare's history plays from childhood. At the Mercury Theatre in 1938, with the success of *Julius Caesar* and *The Shoemaker's Holiday* established, Welles thought next of mounting a great festival of drama to be called *Five Kings,* an amalgam of *Richard II, Henry IV, parts 1 & 2, Henry V,* the three *Henry VI* plays, and *Richard III,* to be shown matinee and evening, or two evenings in a row; he had put on such a production at the Todd School when he was fifteen. This plan was shelved, but it came to life again in the wake of the excitement about *The War of the Worlds.* After deciding that the whole cycle was impractical, Welles reduced the scenario to what could be performed in a single evening, still to be called *Five Kings;* but the tryouts in Boston and Philadelphia were so chaotic that the show never opened in New York – the one clear miscalculation of Welles's early career. Through the years, as Welles continued to think about this material, he developed a clearer conception of what really interested him in the cycle, the relations among Henry IV, Hal, and Falstaff, a conception, as he reported to Bogdanovich, which meant a lot to him personally – and this distillation of his life's thinking became the substance of *Chimes at Midnight.* With this film financial exigencies exerted their usual pressure, but another aspect of reality exerted a more fruitful pressure, namely, the exact timetable of shooting that Welles worked out simply because he had to – because Gielgud (in the role of King Henry IV) could give him only so many days, Jeanne Moreau (as Doll Tearsheet) only so many days, and so forth, and these days had to be scheduled in advance. The shooting of *Othello* had often had to await the availability of performers, but that of *Chimes at Midnight* took place under the more usefully focusing imperative of this tight schedule, the benefits of which Welles hadn't experienced since he'd left Hollywood. This poverty had its disadvantages, to be sure, notably in the really grievous blemishes of the soundtrack, out of sync at many points and hard to understand in all the Hotspur (Norman Rodway) scenes, however excitingly they are filmed in the echoing castle. But under these conditions, learning how to manage on minimal resources in many other respects came easily, and produced beautiful, admirable, and unexpected effects.

In the key confrontation scene, for instance, Prince Hal (Keith Baxter) stands rebuked before the king in the middle of ordinary half-ruined vernacular architecture, some stone columns and pilasters, almost randomly placed, and all displayed without splendor. But it's a key image of the film, all the same, and an effective one. The barrenness in which Hal is standing alone has a hint of metaphor, but this isn't really metaphorical, it's just plain and simple, the way it really was; and the undecorated space in which Hal is standing likewise makes a modest and plain image of his condition. There's no heightened rhetoric; the sparse décor speaks for itself.

The great Tewksbury battle scene is a better-known instance of this moderation. From the look of it, the whole long sequence might have been composed in principled relinquishment of high style. One suspects another motive – we may have caught Welles at an un-Wellesian moment here, making do with whatever energy remained to him. For a battle scene might be dangerous to make. Welles had injured himself more than once in reckless service to the theater, and though he was certainly one to be proud of his daring, such risks must now have passed well beyond even his physical strength, and common sense would have told him, if asked, that such risks ought to have passed beyond even the dreams of an overweight, fifty-one-year-old, heavy overeater and drinker. But the overindulgent Welles remained a practical man of the theater to the end. The director who laid out the Tewksbury battle scene was a complete engineer of the logistical and dynamic aspects of film; whatever his own physical condition, he knew what resources and instruments he still commanded and which of them still worked. And he liked what he had achieved with these resources in the battle scene, if we can thus interpret his setting the whole battle episode slightly apart from the rest of the film, putting it stylistically in a special and distinct realm. Battles have to be noisy, but the moments of life and death at Tewksbury, fully registered as they are, aren't noisy. The whole sequence, far from competing with Olivier's battle in *Henry V,* offers instead a sober, realistic, nonheroic, record of the deaths of men in war.

Welles had mounted parts of the history plays before at key points in his career, starting at the earliest conceivable moment, when, at the age of fifteen, in his last year at the Todd School, he had expanded *Richard III* into the extravaganza of *Five Kings,* cut and pasted from Shakespeare's entire English history cycle – a sort of graduation present for his teachers and friends, and for himself, its very young director, now completing his reign as the school's boy genius. With this production Welles began a structure he was to complete only at the other end of his career, in the film we're discussing now. Here he balanced what may have been quite immature early attempts at Shakespeare's histories with a fully matured and now very intelligently slimmed-down redaction of the whole cycle of the Henry plays, which he called *Chimes at Midnight.*

The abundant Wellesian magic in this film takes the form not of theatrical transformations but of the astonishing freshness with which Welles conjured up some precious but familiar material. There is the tenderness of nostalgia here, a quality we don't associate with Welles. The intense charm of the opening is dangerously eager to be liked – which Welles had rarely been before – and yet it works, the spontaneity of its feeling is solid and true. Falstaff and Shallow (Alan Webb) are coming toward us riding slowly down their little hill, reminiscing about listening to the chimes at midnight when they were young blades in the Inns of Court; they think and speak directly about life and death, dying and living, and what they say is as marvelously fresh on Welles's screen as it still is in Shakespeare's *Henry IV, part* 2 (III.ii), where Welles found (and rearranged) these lines for his movie's prologue:

> JUSTICE SHALLOW: Jesus, the days that we have seen. . . . Do you remember since we lay all night in the Windmill, in St George's Field?
> FALSTAFF: No more of that, Master Shallow.

Such open, unironic, ingenuous writing – which targets the sentiment so exactly – almost justifies Harold Bloom's witty remark that it was Shake-

Prince Hal (Keith Baxter) stands rebuked before the king (John Gielgud). (Photo courtesy of Photofest)

speare who invented human nature, for he does miraculously make us hear this sentiment and these words as if for the first time. And when to the words is added the tact with which Welles directs the little procession winding over the snow, the effect pierces one's heart as deeply as it must have touched Welles's – as deeply as art had ever touched him before, perhaps, if we can trust the depth of emotion we read on Falstaff's face at this moment. Nostalgia and charm are not the noblest reaches of art, but they can be marvelously infectious and humanizing, and when Falstaff's face answers Shallow's "Jesus, the days that we have seen" with generously expressive acknowledgment, the feeling is so ordinary, yet so intimate and so intense, that we seem to be watching the character himself, perhaps Welles himself, consider what his own career had been and could have been. Such open expressivity returns in the sublime last images of the film, with Falstaff left behind by the coronation procession, in distraught and deeply suffering rejection. In this scene, and elsewhere in the film too, Welles wears no mask, he suffers behind no persona; the emotion he is expressing is unmediated, the thing itself. And yet the ex-

Gielgud and Baxter as royal father and son at the great battle of Tewksbury. (Photo courtesy of Photofest)

cruciating effect remains mild and quiet, like the whole film. In Falstaff's agonizing realization that Hal has rejected him, one suffers with the force and weight of Welles's empathy with the character, but there is no heaviness.

The unity in the whole of *Chimes at Midnight* seems as if the script had been written all in one resourceful key. Much of this rare effect undoubtedly comes from Welles's stroke of genius in casting John Gielgud as King Henry IV. After the 1950s, Welles occasionally brought into his productions certain actors from outside his company – partly out of friendship, partly for Great Theater, partly for show business, partly for necessity. Very little of his old company remained; he himself had taken to performing brilliant cameos in other directors' films – as Cardinal Woolsey in Fred Zinnemann's *A Man for All Seasons,* as Clarence Darrow in Richard Fleischer's *Compulsion,* and other roles that suited his manner, his temperament, and his bulk.

When reciprocation was in order, he extended two inspired invitations, to Dietrich in *Touch of Evil* and to Gielgud in *Chimes at Midnight*

"Late-period music": Baxter's Hal, Welles's Falstaff. (Photo courtesy of Photofest)

– mighty magicians indeed, for the transformative power of these guest artists must have outstripped whatever Welles had planned.

The importation of John Gielgud led to a more sustained sound, a more pervasive transformation than Dietrich could work on the rest of *Touch of Evil.* This magic enabled Welles to present, so it seems, the whole triangle of power in *Chimes at Midnight* in the continuous tonality of Gielgud's voice. When Welles got Gielgud to play Henry IV, he acquired something that could have proved hard to handle for a less venturesome director – the intensely inward Gielgud voice, which admittedly is hard at first to associate with the outgoing manly force of Bolingbroke. But Gielgud's vocal power, however different in timbre, easily matches in tensile strength the power one expects from Bolingbroke, and he projects this line of sound strongly enough to pervade the whole film with as special a flavor as Dietrich's presence had given to *Touch of Evil.*

What Gielgud brings to the ensemble is the steady aching burden of his melancholy voice – touching, on the one hand, formal threnody; on the other, an emotion so close to self-pity that it would be embarrassing to listen to were it not for the actor's almost magical control over it even at this pitch of lachrymose song.

After Gielgud's midcareer one began to hear more distinctly the pathos of the vocal signature he had practiced so long – singing it over and over again, in role after role, both serious and comic – that pathos so readily identifiable as his, so poignantly near to strain, that almost strangled, high-tenor lament that speaks his delicate taste and tells us of the pathos of his isolation, which is so closely linked to his eloquently ravaged face and has the same meaning.

We don't know how deliberately Welles meant to focus on Gielgud's voice – some of the effect seems inadvertent, though not the less effective for that. It doesn't quite answer the question to note that Hal, Hotspur, and Falstaff were all allowed to join the game of imitating Gielgud's voice, in mild, affectionate mockery of Gielgud himself, a round of imitations that augments the sound and the power of Gielgud's voice as a factor in the film's structure.

The note of threnody in Gielgud's voice might be painfully overinsistent but for the flexibility of the vocal training in the English drama schools and in the theaters themselves; training in which he had learned how to enact purpose and motive by means of the continuity with which he deploys his voice. Welles asked Gielgud to go to the top of his discipline for this sublime late-period music, and Gielgud didn't disappoint him.

Macbeth and *Othello* are about the passions – political, social, and sexual – of people in their prime of life, with strong minds and strong bodies. *Chimes at Midnight* is about age, the loss of strength, the disappointments of achieved power. It's right, then, that *Chimes at Midnight* stands apart from Welles's other work: in its mildness and moderation, its lack of the pressure of deliberate brilliance and flair. If Welles had been a composer, *Chimes at Midnight* would be his late-period music. His editing style is simple, even ordinary, with hardly a single brilliantly Wellesian stroke. This may not be what the first audience expected or wanted from its genius, but it's a beautiful and admirable achievement in itself and makes excellent sense as the last move in a restless career.

Notes

1. Career Overview

1. Quoted by Pauline Kael in “Raising Kane,” in *The Citizen Kane Book* (Boston: Little, Brown & Company, 1971), 3–84, at 84.
2. Bernard Shaw, *Shaw’s Music: The Complete Musical Criticism*, 3 vols, Dan H. Laurence, ed. (New York: Dodd, Mead & Co., 1981), 2:761–2.
3. Simon Callow, *Orson Welles: The Road to Xanadu* (New York: Viking, 1995), 46.
4. Barbara Leaming, *Orson Welles* (New York: Viking, 1985), 241.
5. Micheál Mac Liammóir, *All for Hecuba: An Irish Theatrical Autobiography* [1946] (Boston: Branden Press, 1967), 129.
6. John Houseman, *Run-Through* (New York: Simon & Schuster, 1972), 193–4.
7. Leaming, *Orson Welles*, 92–3.
8. Orson Welles and Peter Bogdanovich, *This Is Orson Welles*, ed. Jonathan Rosenbaum (New York: Harper Collins, 1992).
9. Leaming, *Orson Welles*, 381.
10. Kael, “Raising Kane,” 73.

2. *Citizen Kane*

1. Pauline Kael, “Raising Kane,” in *The Citizen Kane Book* (Boston: Little, Brown & Company, 1971), 3–84, at 4. Subsequent citations in this chapter are given by page number in the text. The script of *Citizen Kane* cited here is the “RKO Cutting Continuity of the Orson Welles Production, *Citizen Kane*,” dated Feb. 21, 1941, in *The Citizen Kane Book*, 307–423.

3. *The Magnificent Ambersons*

1. Tarkington’s original reads, “So, whatever we are, we must have been in the sun.” Booth Tarkington, *The Magnificent Ambersons* [1918] (Bloomington: Indiana University Press, 1989), 428–9.
2. Robert L. Carringer, *“The Magnificent Ambersons”: A Reconstruction* (Berkeley: University of California Press, 1993), 281–4.

3. Orson Welles and Peter Bogdanovich, *This Is Orson Welles,* ed. Jonathan Rosenbaum (New York: Harper Collins, 1992), 126.

4. *The Lady from Shanghai*

1. Orson Welles and Peter Bogdanovich, *This Is Orson Welles,* ed. Jonathan Rosenbaum (New York: Harper Collins, 1992), 187.
2. Ibid., 198.
3. The term had originated in essays in 1946 by French critics Nino Frank and Jean-Pierre Chartier but was not widely adopted until later.

5. *Touch of Evil*

1. Barbara Leaming, *Orson Welles* (New York: Viking, 1985), 422–3.
2. David Thomson, *Rosebud: The Story of Orson Welles* (New York: Alfred A. Knopf, Inc., 1996), 337.

6. Welles's Shakespeare

1. Quotations from Shakespeare's plays refer by act, scene, and line numbers within the text to *The Riverside Shakespeare,* gen. ed. G. Blakemore Evans, with Harry Levin, Herschel Baker, and Charles H. Shattuck (Boston: Houghton Mifflin, 1974).
2. Welles postpones the first half of the soliloquy (1–12) – from "If it were done . . ." to "To our own lips" – until after the prayer is concluded. The rest of line 12 ("He's here in double trust") to line 16 ("Besides, this Duncan") is cut altogether from the film.

Bibliography

Callow, Simon. *Orson Welles: The Road to Xanadu*. New York: Viking, 1995.

Carringer, Robert L. *"The Magnificent Ambersons": A Reconstruction*. Berkeley: University of California Press, 1993.

Evans, G. Blakemore, gen. ed., with Harry Levin, Herschel Baker, and Charles H. Shattuck. *The Riverside Shakespeare*. Boston: Houghton Mifflin, 1974.

Houseman, John. *Run-Through*. New York: Simon & Schuster, 1972.

Kael, Pauline. "Raising Kane," in *The Citizen Kane Book*. Boston: Little, Brown & Company, 1971, pp. 3–84.

Leaming, Barbara. *Orson Welles*. New York: Viking, 1985.

Mac Liammóir, Micheál. *All for Hecuba: An Irish Theatrical Autobiography*. [1946.] Boston: Branden Press, 1967.

Shaw, Bernard. *Shaw's Music: The Complete Musical Criticism*. 3 vols. Dan H. Laurence, ed. New York: Dodd, Mead & Co., 1981.

Thomson, David. *Rosebud: The Story of Orson Welles*. New York: Alfred A. Knopf; distributed by Random House, Inc., 1996.

Welles, Orson, and Peter Bogdanovich. *This Is Orson Welles*. Edited by Jonathan Rosenbaum. New York: Harper Collins, 1992.

Filmography

Note: Unless otherwise indicated, years given are release dates.

Citizen Kane (1941)

DIR: Orson Welles; SCR: Herman J. Mankiewicz, Orson Welles (and John Houseman, uncredited); PROD: Orson Welles; PH: Gregg Toland, ORIG MUSIC: Bernard Herrmann; ED: Robert Wise; ART DIR: Van Nest Polglase; SET DECOR: Darrell Silvera; PROD CO: Mercury Productions/RKO Radio Pictures; bw, 1.37:1, 119 min; DVD: Warner, Arthaus, Universal; LASERDISC: Criterion, Image

CAST: Orson Welles (Charles Foster Kane), Joseph Cotten (Jedediah Leland), Dorothy Comingore (Susan Alexander Kane), Agnes Moorehead (Mrs. Mary Kane), Ruth Warrick (Emily Monroe Norton Kane), Ray Collins (Boss James "Jim" W. Gettys), Erskine Sanford (Herbert Carter, *Inquirer* Editor-in-Chief), Everett Sloane (Mr. Bernstein), William Alland (Jerry Thompson/*News on the March* narrator), Paul Stewart (Raymond, Kane's butler), George Coulouris (Walter Parks Thatcher), Fortunio Bonanova (Signor Matiste), Gus Schilling (headwaiter), Philip Van Zandt (Mr. Rawlston), Georgia Backus (Miss Bertha Anderson), Harry Shannon (Kane's father), Sonny Bupp (Charles Foster Kane III), Buddy Swan (Kane, age eight)

The Magnificent Ambersons (1942)

DIR: Orson Welles; SCR: Orson Welles (after Booth Tarkington novel); PROD: Orson Welles; PH: Stanley Cortez; ORIG MUSIC: Bernard Herrmann; ED: Robert Wise; PROD DES: Albert S. D'Agostino; PROD CO: Mercury Productions/RKO Radio Pictures; bw, 1.37:1, 88 min; LASERDISC: Criterion

CAST: Orson Welles (Narrator), Joseph Cotten (Eugene), Dolores Costello (Isabel), Anne Baxter (Lucy), Tim Holt (George), Agnes Moorehead (Fanny), Ray Collins (Jack), Erskine Sanford (Roger Bronson), Richard Bennett (Maj. Amberson)

Journey into Fear (1942)

DIR: Norman Foster, Orson Welles (uncredited); SCR: Joseph Cotten (and Ben Hecht, Orson Welles, uncredited) (after Eric Ambler novel); PROD: Orson Welles; PH: Karl Struss; ORIG MUSIC: Roy Webb; ED: Mark Robson; ART DIR: Albert S. D'Agostino, Mark-Lee Kirk; SET DECOR: Ross Dowd, Darrell Silvera; PROD CO: Mercury Productions/RKO Radio Pictures; bw, 1.37:1, 71 min

CAST: Joseph Cotten (Howard Graham), Dolores del Rio (Josette Martel, nightclub singer), Ruth Warrick (Stephanie Graham), Agnes Moorehead (Mrs. Mathews), Orson Welles (Colonel Haki, head of Turkish Secret Police), Jack Durant (Gogo Martel), Everett Sloane (Kopeikin, Bainbridge & Son Armaments representative), Eustace Wyatt (Dr. Haller, German archeologist/Mueller, Nazi agent/Bill Ridgley, representative of Graham's company), Frank Readick (Matthews), Edgar Barrier (Kuvetli, Turkish agent [tobacco salesman]), Jack Moss (Peter Banat, Nazi agent), Stefan Schnabel (Purser), Hans Conried (Oo Lang Sang, nightclub magician), Robert Meltzer (Steward), Richard Bennett (ship's captain)

The Stranger (1946)

DIR: Orson Welles; SCR: Anthony Veiller (and John Huston, Orson Welles, uncredited) (after story by Victor Trivas); PROD: Sam Spiegel (as S.P. Eagle); PH: Russell Metty; ORIG MUSIC: Bronislau (as Bronislaw) Kaper; ED: Ernest J. Nims; PROD DES: Perry Ferguson; ART DIR: Albert S. D'Agostino; PROD CO: International Pictures/RKO Radio Pictures/Haig Corporation; bw, 1.37:1, 95 min; DVD: Master Movies

CAST: Orson Welles (Dr. Charles Rankin/Franz Kindler), Edward G. Robinson (Mr. Wilson), Loretta Young (Mary Longstreet), Philip Merivale (Judge Longstreet), Richard Long (Noah Longstreet), Konstantin Shayne (Konrad Meinike), Byron Keith (Dr. Jeff Lawrence), Billy House (Mr. Potter), Martha Wentworth (Sara)

The Lady from Shanghai (1948)

DIR: Orson Welles; SCR: Orson Welles (and William Castle, Charles Lederer, Fletcher Markle, uncredited) (after Sherwood King novel *If I Die before I Wake*); PROD: Orson Welles; PH: Charles Lawton Jr.; ORIG MUSIC: Heinz Roemheld; ED: Viola Lawrence; ART DIR: Sturges Carne, Stephen Goosson; SET DECOR: Wilbur Menefee, Herman Schoenbrun; PROD CO: Mercury Productions/Columbia Pictures; bw, 1.37:1, 87 min; DVD: Columbia/Tristar; LASERDISC: RCA/Columbia

CAST: Rita Hayworth (Mrs. Elsa "Rosalie" Bannister) (singing voice: Anita Ellis), Orson Welles (Michael O'Hara aka Black Irish/Narrator), Everett Sloane (Arthur Bannister), Glenn Anders (George Grisby, Bannister's law partner), Ted de Corsia (Sidney Broome, Bannister's butler), Erskine Sanford (judge), Gus Schilling ("Goldie" Goldfish), Carl Frank (District Attorney Galloway), Louis Merrill (Jake), Evelyn Ellis (Bessie, Bannister's maid/cook), Harry Shannon (cab driver), Errol Flynn (extra [aboard yacht])

Macbeth (1948)

DIR: Orson Welles; SCR: William Shakespeare (adapted by Orson Welles); PROD: Orson Welles; PH: John L. Russell; ORIG MUSIC: Jacques Ibert; ED: Louis Lindsay; ART DIR: Fred A. Ritter; SET DECOR: John McCarthy Jr., James Redd; PROD CO: Mercury Productions/Republic Pictures/Literary Classics Productions; bw, 1.37:1, 89 min (107 restored); LASERDISC: Republic, Image

CAST: Orson Welles (Macbeth), Jeanette Nolan (Lady Macbeth), Dan O'Herlihy (Macduff), Roddy McDowall (Malcolm), Edgar Barrier (Banquo), Alan Napier (Holy Father), Erskine Sanford (Duncan), John Dierkes (Ross), Keene Curtis (Lennox), Peggy Webber (Lady Macduff/Witch), Lionel Braham (Siward), Archie Heugly (Young Siward), Jerry Farber (Fleance), Christopher Welles (Macduff child), Morgan Farley (Doctor), Lurene Tuttle (First gentlewoman/Witch), Brainerd Duffield (First murderer/Witch), William Alland (Second murderer), George Chirello (Seyton), Gus Schilling (Porter)

Othello (aka *The Tragedy of Othello: The Moor of Venice*) (1952)

DIR: Orson Welles; SCR: William Shakespeare (adapted by Orson Welles and Jean Sacha); PROD: Orson Welles; PH: Anchise Brizzi, George Fanto, Alberto Fusi, Aldo Graziati (as G. R. Aldo), Oberdan Troiani; ORIG MUSIC: Angelo Francesco Lavagnino, Alberto Barberis; ED: Jenö Csepreghy (as John Shepridge), Renzo Lucidi, William Morton, Jean Sacha; PROD DES: Luigi Scaccianoce, Alexandre Trauner; PROD CO: Mercury Productions; bw, 1.37:1, 90 min; LASERDISC: Criterion

CAST: Orson Welles (Othello), Micheál Mac Liammóir (Iago), Robert Coote (Roderigo), Suzanne Cloutier (Desdemona), Hilton Edwards (Brabantio), Nicholas Bruce (Lodovico), Michael Laurence (Michael Cassio), Fay Compton (Emilia), Doris Dowling (Bianca); *uncredited:* Abdullah Ben Mohamet (page-boy), Joseph Cotten (Senator), Jean Davis (Montano), Joan Fontaine (page)

Mr. Arkadin (aka *Confidential Report; Mister Arkadin*) (1955)

DIR: Orson Welles; SCR: Orson Welles; PROD: Orson Welles; PH: Jean Bourgoin; ORIG MUSIC: Paul Misraki; ED: Renzo Lucidi; ART DIR: Orson Welles (uncredited); PROD CO: Mercury Productions/Cervantes Films/Filmorsa (as Film Organization S.A.)/Sevilla Films; bw, 1.37:1, 93 min; DVD: Laserlight; LASERDISC: Criterion, Pioneer Cinema

CAST: Akim Tamiroff (Jakob Zouk), Grégoire Aslan (Bracco), Patricia Medina (Mily), Jack Watling (Marquis of Rutleigh), Orson Welles (Gregory

Arkadin), Mischa Auer (Professor), Peter van Eyck (Thaddeus), Michael Redgrave (Burgomil Trebitsch), Suzanne Flon (Baroness Nagel), Frédéric O'Brady (Oscar), Katina Paxinou (Sophie), Tamara Shayne (as Shane) (woman in apartment), Paola Mori (Raina Arkadin), Robert Arden (Guy Van Stratten), Terence Longdon (Secretary), Annabel (Parisian woman with bread), Gert Fröbe (Policeman), Eduard Linkers (as Linker) (Man), Manuel Requen (General Martinez)

Touch of Evil (1958)

DIR: Orson Welles; SCR: Orson Welles (and Paul Monash, uncredited) (after Whit Masterson novel *Badge of Evil*); PROD: Albert Zugsmith; PH: Russell Metty; ORIG MUSIC: Henry Mancini; ED: Virgil Vogel; ART DIR: Robert Clatworthy, Alexander Golitzen; SET DECOR: John P. Austin, Russell A. Gausman; PROD CO: Universal International Pictures; bw, 1.37:1), 95 min (USA restored 105); DVD: Universal (1.85:1 "director's cut" 111); LASERDISC: Pioneer Cinema

CAST: Charlton Heston (Ramon Miguel "Mike" Vargas), Janet Leigh (Susan "Susie" Vargas), Orson Welles (Capt. Hank Quinlan), Joseph Calleia (Sgt. Pete Menzies), Akim Tamiroff (Uncle Joe Grandi), Joanna [Cook] Moore (Marcia Linnekar), Ray Collins (District Attorney Adair), Dennis Weaver (motel night manager), Valentin de Vargas (Pancho), Mort Mills (Al Schwartz, District Attorney's office), Victor Millan (Manelo Sanchez), Lalo Rios (Risto, acid thrower), Michael Sargent (Boy), Phil Harvey (Blaine), Joi Lansing (blonde), Harry Shannon (Chief Gould), Marlene Dietrich (Tanya), Zsa Zsa Gabor (nightclub owner), Joseph Cotten (police surgeon), Mercedes McCambridge (gang leader)

The Trial (1962)

DIR: Orson Welles; SCR: Orson Welles (after Franz Kafka novel); PROD: Alexander and Michael Salkind; PH: Edmond Richard; ORIG MUSIC: Jean Ledrut; ED: Yvonne Martin, Frederick (as Fritz H.) Muller; ART DIR: Jean Mandaroux; PROD CO: Paris-Europa Productions / FI-C-IT / Hisa-Film; bw, 1.66:1, 118 min; DVD: Image Entertainment; LASERDISC: Roan Group

CAST: Anthony Perkins (Josef K.), Orson Welles (Hastler), Arnoldo Foà (Inspector A), Jess Hahn (second assistant inspector), Billy Kearns (first assistant inspector), Madeleine Robinson (Mrs. Grubach), Jeanne Moreau (Miss Burstner), Maurice Teynac (deputy manager), Naydra Shore (Irmie, Josef K.'s cousin), Suzanne Flon (Miss Pittl), Raoul Delfosse (policeman), Jean-Claude Rémoleux (policeman), Max Buchsbaum (examining magistrate), Carl Studer (man in leather), Max Haufler (Uncle Max), Romy Schneider (Leni), Fernand Ledoux (chief clerk of the law court), Akim Tamiroff (Bloch), Elsa Martinelli (Hilda), Thomas Holtzmann (Bert, law student), Wolfgang Reichmann (courtroom guard), William Chappell (Titorelli), Michael Lonsdale (priest)

Chimes at Midnight (aka *Falstaff*) (1966)

DIR: Orson Welles; SCR: Orson Welles (after William Shakespeare plays *Henry IV, Parts I & II; Henry V; Richard III; The Merry Wives of Windsor;* and Raphael Holinshed's *Chronicles of England, Scotlande, and Irelande*); PROD: Alessandro Tasca; PH: Edmond Richard; ORIG MUSIC: Angelo Francesco Lavagnino; ED: Elena Jaumandreu, Frederick (as Fritz) Muller, Peter Parasheles; SET DECOR: José Antonio de la Guerra; PROD CO: Internacional Films Española/Alpine Films; bw, 1.37:1, 115 min; DVD: Suevia Films

CAST: Orson Welles (Falstaff), Jeanne Moreau (Doll Tearsheet), Margaret Rutherford (Mistress Quickly), John Gielgud (Henry IV), Marina Vlady (Kate Percy), Walter Chiari (Silence), Michael Aldridge (Pistol), Tony Beckley (Ned Poins), Jeremy Rowe (Prince John), Alan Webb (Shallow), Fernando Rey (Worcester), Keith Baxter (Prince Hal), Norman Rodway (Henry "Hotspur" Percy), José Nieto (Northumberland), Andrew Faulds (Westmoreland), Patrick Bedford (Bardolph), Beatrice Welles (Falstaff's page), Ralph Richardson (narrator)

The Immortal Story (1968)

DIR: Orson Welles; SCR: Orson Welles, Louise de Vilmorin (after Isak Dinesen novella); PROD: Micheline Rozan; PH: Willy Kurant; ED: Claude Farny, Françoise Garnault, Yolande Maurette, Marcelle Pluet; PROD CO: ORTF/ Albina Productions S.a.r.l.; color, 58 min; VHS: Connoisseur Video

CAST: Jeanne Moreau (Virginie Ducrot), Orson Welles (Mr. Charles Clay) (dubbed into French by Philippe Noiret), Roger Coggio (Elishama Levinsky), Norman Eshley (Paul, sailor), Fernando Rey (Merchant)

F for Fake (1975)

DIR: Orson Welles; SCR: Orson Welles, Oja Kodar (as Oja Palinkas); PROD: François Reichenbach; PH: Gary Graver, Christian Odasso; ORIG MUSIC: Michel Legrand; ED: Marie-Sophie Dubus, Dominique Engerer; PROD CO: Janus Film/Les Films de l'Astrophore/SACI; color, 85 min; LASERDISC: Criterion

CAST: Orson Welles (Himself), Oja Kodar (Girl), Joseph Cotten, François Reichenbach, Richard Wilson, Paul Stewart, Sasa Devcic, Gary Graver, Andrés Vicente Gómez, Julio Palinkas, Christian Odasso, Françoise Widhoff, Peter Bogdanovich, William Alland

Unfinished

It's All True (unfinished in 1942)

Don Quixote (unfinished in 1955)

The Deep (aka *Dead Reckoning*) (unfinished in 1970)

The Other Side of the Wind (unfinished in 1972)

Jane Eyre (1944)

DIR: Robert Stevenson; SCR: John Houseman, Aldous Huxley, Robert Stevenson; PROD: William Goetz; PROD CO: Twentieth Century–Fox; bw, 97 min
CAST: Orson Welles (Edward Rochester), Joan Fontaine (Jane Eyre), Margaret O'Brien (Adele Varens), Agnes Moorehead (Mrs. Reed)

Tomorrow Is Forever (1946)

DIR: Irving Pichel; SCR: Lenore J. Coffee; PROD: David Lewis; PROD CO: International Pictures; bw, 105 min
CAST: Claudette Colbert (Elizabeth Hamilton), Orson Welles (John Andrew MacDonald/Erik Kessler), George Brent (Lawrence "Larry" Hamilton)

The Third Man (1949)

DIR: Carol Reed; SCR: Graham Greene; PROD: Carol Reed; PROD CO: British Lion Film/London Film; bw, 104 min
CAST: Joseph Cotten (Holly Martins), Alida Valli (Anna Schmidt), Orson Welles (Harry Lime), Trevor Howard (Major Calloway)

Prince of Foxes (1949)

DIR: Henry King; SCR: Milton Krims; PROD: Sol C. Siegel; PROD CO: Twentieth Century–Fox; bw, 107 min
CAST: Tyrone Power (Andrea Orsini), Orson Welles (Cesare Borgia), Marina Berti (Angela Borgia), Everett Sloane (Mario Belli)

The Black Rose (1950)

DIR: Henry Hathaway; SCR: Talbot Jennings; PROD: Louis D. Lighton; PROD CO: Twentieth Century–Fox; color, 120 min
CAST: Tyrone Power (Walter of Gurnie), Orson Welles (Bayan), Cécile Aubry (Maryam), Jack Hawkins (Tritram Griffin), Michael Rennie (Edward)

Compulsion (1959)

DIR: Richard Fleischer; SCR: Richard Murphy, Meyer Levin; PROD: Richard D. Zanuck; PROD CO: Twentieth Century–Fox; bw, 103 min
CAST: Orson Welles (Jonathan Wilk), Dean Stockwell (Judd Steiner), Bradford Dillman (Artie Straus), E. G. Marshall (District Attorney Horn)

A Man for All Seasons (1966)

DIR: Fred Zinnemann; SCR: Robert Bolt; PROD: Fred Zinnemann; PROD CO: Open Road; color, 120 min
CAST: Paul Scofield (Thomas More), Wendy Hiller (Alice More), Leo McKern (Thomas Cromwell), Robert Shaw (Henry VIII), Orson Welles (Cardinal Wolsey)

Non-Welles Films Cited

Alexander Nevsky (1938) DIR: Sergei M. Eisenstein, Dmitri Vasilyev; PROD CO: Mosfil'm

Around the World in Eighty Days (1956); DIR: Michael Anderson; PROD: Michael Todd; PROD CO: Michael Todd Company/United Artists

The Big Sleep (1946); DIR: Howard Hawks; PROD: Howard Hawks; PROD CO: First National Pictures/Warner Bros.

Christmas Holiday (1944), DIR: Robert Siodmak; PROD: Felix Jackson; PROD CO: Universal Pictures

Criss Cross (1949); DIR: Robert Siodmak; PROD: Michael Kraike; PROD CO: Universal International Pictures

Cry of the City (1948); DIR: Robert Siodmak; PROD: Sol C. Siegel; PROD CO: Twentieth Century–Fox

Double Indemnity (1944); DIR: Billy Wilder; PROD: Buddy G. DeSylva; PROD CO: Paramount Pictures

8½ (aka *Otto e mezzo*) (1963); DIR: Federico Fellini; PROD: Angelo Rizzoli; PROD CO: Cineriz/Francinex

The File on Thelma Jordon (1950); DIR: Robert Siodmak; PROD: Hal B. Wallis; PROD CO: Paramount Pictures

The Grapes of Wrath (1940); DIR: John Ford; PROD: Darryl F. Zanuck; PROD CO: Twentieth Century–Fox

Henry V (aka *Henry the Fifth*) (1944) [USA, 1946]; DIR: Laurence Olivier, PROD: Laurence Olivier, Fillippo Del Guidice; PROD CO: Two Cities Film/Eagle–Lion

Ivan the Terrible (*Ivan Groznyi*), pts. I–II (1945/1958 [shot 1944–6]), DIR: Sergei M. Eisenstein (and M. Filimonova, pt. II); PROD: Sergei M. Eisenstein; PROD CO: TsOKS/Alma-Ata Studio

The Killers (aka *A Man Alone*) (1946); DIR: Robert Siodmak; PROD: Mark Hellinger; PROD CO: Mark Hellinger Productions/Universal Pictures

Mad Love (aka *The Hands of Orlac*) (1935); DIR: Karl Freund; PROD: John W. Considine Jr.; PROD CO: MGM

Monsieur Verdoux (1947); DIR: Charles Chaplin; PROD: Charles Chaplin; PROD CO: Chaplin/United Artists

Othello (1965); DIR: Stuart Burge, John Dexter; PROD: BHE Films; PROD CO: Warner Bros.

Out of the Past (aka *Build My Gallows High*) (1947); DIR: Jacques Tourneur; PROD: Warren Duff; PROD CO: RKO Radio Pictures

Pitfall (1948); DIR: André de Toth; PROD: Samuel Bischoff; PROD CO: Regal Films/United Artists

The Power and the Glory (1933); DIR: William K. Howard; PROD: Jesse L. Lasky; PROD CO: Fox Film

The Reckless Moment (1949); DIR: Max Ophüls; PROD: Walter Wanger; PROD CO: Columbia Pictures

Stagecoach (1939); DIR: John Ford; PROD: Walter Wanger, John Ford; PROD CO: Wanger Prods./United Artists

Index

Note: Page numbers in bold italics indicate illustrations. Works listed are films and by Welles unless otherwise noted.